Knowing Will Charlick

Lucy Staunton

Copyright © 2022 Lucy Staunton

ISBN: 9781918264340

All rights reserved, including the right to reproduce this book, or portions thereof in any form. No part of this text may be reproduced, transmitted, downloaded, decompiled, reverse engineered, or stored, in any form or introduced into any information storage and retrieval system, in any form or by any means, whether electronic or mechanical without the express written permission of the author.

This is a work of fiction. Names and characters are the product of the author's imagination and any resemblance to actual persons, living or dead, is entirely coincidental.

The views expressed in this work are solely those of the author and do not necessarily reflect the views of the publisher, and the publisher hereby disclaims any responsibility for them.

www.publishnation.co.uk

Stephill Hospital, Wednesday 6th November 1974

'That's it Mrs Charlick, or may I call you Evelyn? Just try and take some deep breaths, as the baby is starting to get a bit distressed,' said the senior midwife, who had just been called into the delivery suite.

'Distressed! I'm about to have a bloody nervous breakdown!' snapped Evelyn. 'Henry, how can this be happening?! We have a dinner and awards ceremony tonight with very important people. Jesus Christ, how can I be having a baby?' she exclaimed, taking another deep breath. 'Haven't had a period for ten months and put on a bit of weight, so assumed it had to be the menopause. Good god that hurts!' she exclaimed again, gripping Henry's hand. 'We don't have time for children, do we Henry? And you can call me Mrs Charlick.' Henry just sat dumbfounded, saying nothing whilst his hand was being crushed.

And with that, William arrived at 6.43am on 6th November 1974, weighing 6lb1oz...

And seven days later William left the hospital, bundled up in the arms of Nanny Mabel.

Mabel and William were both introduced to their new life abruptly, with Evelyn announcing, 'There are a few rules that I need to lay down straight away: Firstly, William will stay in your bedroom with you at night until he is sleeping well; running our own business means it is very important we get a good nights' sleep. Secondly, our hours are long with very few days off, so yours will have to be the same. Thirdly, a book has been put in the hall for you to detail the events of each day; failure to do this will result in reduced wages. Your wages will be paid in cash every Friday and will be left in the book. I take it you won't have any problems with this.'

'No, I'm sure that will be fine,' replied Mabel, cradling little William in her arms.

At sixty-eight years old, he couldn't have wished for a more loving, caring and delightful person to nurture and raise him. Evelyn was also delighted with her choice; William was growing into a charming young boy who everyone that she showed him to adored (and she of course took a lot of the credit for that) much to the amusement of Mabel but more importantly to her, Henry definitely didn't fancy her. She had heard enough stories about husbands and nannies!

So life continued happily, with Evelyn and Henry putting in an appearance in William's world when it was convenient or advantageous and Mabel loving every second she had with him. From the sleepless nights and teething, to first words and steps, Mabel was always the first to experience everything. Of course, she let Evelyn believe that when she experienced whatever milestone it was, it was the first time Will had done it and should really have been awarded an Oscar for being so convincing. From walking and talking, to learning to swim and ride a bike, Mabel was always by his side, supporting and encouraging him that 'you can do it' whilst clapping, and swinging him around in the air when he finally mastered it! She had all the time in the world for Will.

Each week she received her so called 'wages'. 'You don't need much as we are paying for all your living costs and not even charging you rent,' said Evelyn, handing her the envelope at the end of her first week. 'Ten pounds should be plenty. I am surprised you are looking like that!' Mabel was shocked. Working round the clock, with no set day off, this seemed so little. She had been struggling on her small pension to cover her council house bills, so was pleased to be able to give notice and move out, but this seemed so measly. Still, she had a dear little boy to raise that needed her so that was more important.

Very rarely did she have any time off as Evelyn and Henry seemed to sleep, work or be 'entertaining' at weekends. So with the wages she had, she and Will decided Saturday night was cinema night. His parents were always at a dinner somewhere, so in the afternoon they would walk down to the local video shop, choose their film and pop into the newsagent to buy their supplies. They especially loved these evenings; sat together on the sofa, curtains drawn to make it as dark as possible, volume up loud. The side table would have bowls with their sweets, crisps and popcorn on and they took it in turns to refill both their bowls, grinning at each other as they sat back down.

At primary school, he made a best friend in James and they regularly spent time after school together. 'Cor, look at your house!' exclaimed James, the first time he went for a play and tea. 'You must be really rich, you are so lucky!' Dropping their bags on the floor and flying up the stairs to Will's bedroom, Mabel beamed with delight as she picked them up and got their drinks and homemade cookies ready to take up. 'I just love this little boy so much,' she muttered to herself.

The dread they both felt if Evelyn got wind that Will was having friends over for tea. It was even worse with organising his birthday parties. She would splash out on all the most expensive cakes, modelling kits for the children to make, party entertainers, cinema trips and always looked very pleased with herself too, showing off to all the parents as they arrived to collect their child. But of course, the children much preferred it if she hadn't heard about it and it was just Will and Mabel; playing 'hide and seek' and 'what's the time Mr Wolf?'; making camps and tunnels with quilts and blankets all over the upstairs of the house and then having a picnic inside and of course their legendary Rice Krispie cakes with each child's initial piped in icing on the top, which Will and Mabel loved making together.

Life sadly, can be so cruel.

After twelve years together and a particularly awful day at school, Will unlocked the front door to find Mabel lying on the hall floor. 'Mabel, Mabel!' he called out, gently tapping her face. 'Mabel please, please, wake up! You can't leave me,' he cried taking hold of her hand and stroking her face. Quickly grabbing the phone 'Please ambulance, please hurry! No, she isn't breathing!' And under the caller's instructions, began trying to bring her back to him. But even with the paramedics' best efforts, Mabel left this world and William's world crumbled and fell apart.

'I am so sorry my love, let's phone your mum,' said the paramedic, nestling his head into her shoulder and taking the phone. The paramedics then quietly wheeled Mabel into the ambulance and, checking he would be ok, left. Evelyn arrived thirty minutes later to find William sobbing on the front steps of the house. 'Darling, come come now, what will people think,' she said, ushering him up the steps and into the house, closing the door behind her. 'Now come on you are twelve years old, not a baby. I was thinking of letting her go soon anyway, maybe it's best this way. She would have found it very hard to leave you as I think you ended up being the child she could never have herself.' William ran up to his room and collapsed on his bed. His mum of course didn't follow. Shortly after he heard the front door click and she was gone again.

Later that evening, he was summoned to the dining room to have dinner with them. 'William you know how busy we are with the business taking off and going international. I mean, this house and everything doesn't pay for itself, you do understand don't you? So daddy and I will not be able to suddenly take over Mabel's duties. We have already found a housekeeper who will cook light meals, do the washing and ironing etc. She will be here while you are at school and will leave your dinner each day, ready for you to heat up when you get in, ok?' There was no point in replying, there never was, as they had already decided that was how it was going to be.

Life for Will became very lonely at home; it was like 'groundhog day'. School, homework, playing on his games console, dinner (all on his own), mum and dad arrive home late pissed, stagger through the hall knocking things over and laughing at god knows what. Whispering to be more careful or they might wake William (probably the loudest 'Ssssh' you have ever heard). 'At least we don't get Mabel peering around her door anymore giving us the death stare!' his mum giggled, while Will lay there wondering what he had done wrong and wishing he could have just one more day with her. Luckily he still had James, who had become his one and only true friend. They kept themselves to themselves at school, not fitting into the main cliques: sporty, ridiculously good looking, fantasy war-game nerds or psychos from the local estate. James was great and his parents invited Will into their home regularly. Even more since Mabel had passed.

This went on for over two years before Will arrived home one day from school to find a note propped up against the kettle.

'Dearest William,

We have decided to move to Australia and are on the plane as you read this. As you are aware, the Aussies are very excited about our business and we feel that it would be best if we relocated to establish us Down Under! Didn't want to interrupt your schooling so thought it would be best for you to stay in the UK. You are now 15 years old and definitely old enough to take care of yourself. The housekeeper has gone, and as a parent's duty is to help their children become independent, we feel now is a good time for you to start taking on more responsibility. We of course don't expect you to work as you are still at school, so all household bills will be paid and money will be sent and also put into your account on a regular basis. With the time difference it will be hard to speak often, but let's communicate by letter (far easier) and won't wake each other up. Frozen ready meals will be delivered every month, so you don't have to worry about cooking every day unless you want to of course.

Keep working hard and don't let us down will you.

Best wishes darling, Mummy and Daddy xx

PS. Wouldn't probably mention it at school unless you want to end up in the children's home on that god awful housing estate, ta ta!

'Oh my god, you must be the worst parents! Piss off to Australia then, see if I care!' he screamed out loud and spent the next thirty minutes kicking anything remotely kickable around the house. Flopping down on his bed, he lay looking up at the ceiling at the glow in the dark stars

Mabel had stuck on, so he was never scared of the dark. 'Stupid, stupid bastards!' he cursed, until his heart rate started returning to normal. 'You can stick your stupid frozen meals up your arse too!' It was a few hours before he felt calm enough to go downstairs and start making plans. By midnight, the lounge was now a gaming heaven! Games console on big TV screen, fridge moved next to sofa, seating rearranged and poncey posh furniture for sale in the local newspaper. You had to make the most of it, right?!

James would regularly come over after school and was very envious of the new setup! 'Don't your parents mind it being like this? You are so lucky, no chance in my house,' he asked, tucking into the snacks and fizzy drinks from the fridge whilst waiting for the next game to load.

'Oh they are so busy with the business and spend such little time here, said I could make it my lounge instead of always being in my bedroom. Especially after losing Mabel,' replied Will, and mentioning her name always stopped any more awkward questions.

*

He rarely heard from his parents, just the odd postcard bragging about how fantastic things were going and how life 'down under' was better than they could possibly have hoped for! When they arrived, the same thing always happened – Will read it, ripped it up, shouted lots of swear words and then looking up asked Mabel out loud 'why she had to go.' Will had recently sent them a letter, asking for their handwritten signatures, months of the year and numbers so he could trace them when needed. He had written to them stating:

'While I might be put in a children's home if they found out you weren't here, you would be arrested for child

neglect and abandonment and get sent to prison. Australia doesn't like crims so you would be deported and never allowed back. So you need to get them to me ASAP as school has some documents that need urgently signing by you!'

Their reply arrived incredibly quickly, costing them a fortune which made Will smile.

*

Who knew that shortly another bombshell was about to drop!

'No James, you can't go!'

James' parents had invited Will over to tea and a sleepover, as they had some news to break. James' dad had to relocate with his job which meant they had to move away from the area.

'We are so sorry Will as we have become very fond of you and feel like you are a part of our family. We wouldn't do this unless we really had to, especially as it is GCSE year for James as well,' his mum said, with a tear in her eye.

'Could I come with you, I would be no bother I promise,' pleaded Will, but of course that couldn't happen.

'Sorry Will, but that's just not possible. I do have a massive favour to ask of you though, and am only asking because you are one of the most caring, trustworthy people we know. Hope your parents will be ok with it too but we aren't allowed to take him to our new place,' said James' mum.

So four weeks later, he is stood on their drive waving them off, holding onto a lead.

'Jesus Christ, can my life get any more shit!' he screamed, slamming the front door. But looking down at the new addition to his family, even though it had just peed on the floor, he at last had something to smile about. It was just him and Max now.

Life was definitely busier, with dog walks to fit into the after school gaming schedule and occasional homework, but enjoyable too. He missed James and his family terribly but still got to chat most evenings on the phone. With his parents saying they would be paying all the bills, he made sure it was a decent amount! He just tried to keep his head down, getting on with his schoolwork and bombing home at lunchtime to let the dog out.

There were two particularly good things about having a dog; firstly mum would go completely ballistic if she found out (*'over my dead body are you ever having a filthy, stinky creature living with us here'* she would say), but secondly, and more importantly, you have company and meet lots of different people on walks. Dogs instantly break that invisible barrier, particularly when they are as friendly and gentle as Max.

Bumping into one of the regular dog walkers, Sheila and her little Westie 'Timmy', she was always a kind smiley face to catch you up on what was happening in the area. Most of the time it was the usual community stuff but she had just updated him on something not so good.

'Was thinking about you yesterday, when I heard the news about that dreadful family being moved nearer to us. Kids are awful apparently; think they will be starting at your school.'

'At least I am in my last year now, thank god. There's loads of us in my year too, so here's hoping I dodge them eh!'

Unfortunately he had the pleasure of meeting the three brothers rather too quickly. 'Bloody hell, look at you and where you live,' they said bumping into him one Saturday, leaving the house with Max. 'You must be loaded!' And so began the daily humiliation and pain at school...

'Everything alright Will?' asked Mr Jenkins, his D&T teacher.

'Yes, fine thanks sir,' he replied quickly smoothing down the back of his hair and straightening up his clothes. He had just finished drying his jumper that they'd ripped off him and dunked in the urinals. It still stank but at least it was dry now.

'You can always talk to me you know, if there is anything troubling you.'

Mr Jenkins had always liked Will. He showed a real talent for anything practical and was a genuinely funny, caring, mature person who was good fun to have in the class.

'Parents coming to parents evening this time Will? I should really like to meet them and let them know how well you are doing,' he asked Will at the end of the lesson.

'Probably not sir, with the business doing really well they don't get much time for anything else. You can write to them though if you want?'

'Yes, maybe I will do that,' he replied, walking off down the corridor.

It was only about two weeks later, that Will was having difficulty in metalwork using the drill. Mr Jenkins had noticed a difference in Will recently and looked down to see why he was struggling. Will had a black eye that he could barely see out of, and bruises all over his knuckles from having his fingers repeatedly shut in the toilet door for not bringing enough money again. 'Crikey, what happened to you, pick a fight with Mike Tyson?' Will just carried on looking down. 'Everything ok at home?' enquired Mr Jenkins.

'Home is fine thanks,' he replied, looking thoroughly miserable.

'Anything to do with the new dimshit - I mean wit brothers?' he whispered in his ear.

William didn't reply and carried on looking down at the drill.

Being one of the oldest teachers in the school and about to retire, nothing passed Mr Jenkins. He wasn't stupid and the headteacher was too weak to do anything about it. 'Calling the parents in is a complete waste of time, if they even bothered to turn up! I heard their other headteacher breaking open the champagne when he found out they were moving to us. Good luck, were his words, you are going to need it. Kids from hell!' said Mr Chamberlain.

'So everyone has to suffer do they? Bloody ridiculous if you ask me. Put them in solitary all day every day if you have to, but you can't just allow them to rule the school and do as they please,' replied Mr Jenkins, but it fell on deaf ears of course.

The three brothers came to school every day, stinking of weed, occasionally going to lessons to cause as much disruption as possible and spent break times picking on the rich kids. Knowing Will's family had money, had made him their prime target. Even when he stopped taking in any money, hoping that would make it stop, he would get even more of a kicking. So he couldn't win. However, Mr Jenkins wasn't going to allow this to keep happening...

One morning shortly after, there was a knock at the classroom door. 'Morning Mrs James.'

'Good morning Mr Jenkins, how can we help you?' she asked.

'I need to see Will about something, so please can he come to my classroom at break this morning?'

'Yes of course. William please go and see Mr Jenkins at break, ok?' she replied. Being an English teacher, she always used his full name.

'Fine,' said Will, looking slightly puzzled.

Peering around his door but not seeing Mr Jenkins anywhere, he called out 'Morning sir, it's Will. You ok?'

Falling backwards out of the cupboard with a mass of wires in hand, Mr Jenkins appeared. 'Thanks for coming Will. I wanted to talk to you about something privately, if that's ok. You see, our new headteacher has asked me to produce plans for all the lessons I teach. I mean, I told him *'Bloody hell, I've been teaching for over thirty-five years, if I don't know what I'm doing I should have been booted out long ago. I mean, most of my pupils do well in their exams, at least the ones that can be bothered so I must be teaching it right*!' But apparently, we might be inspected or something, so have to have them ready. Blimmin jobsworths if you ask me, and I've only got two terms left too!'

'Ok sir, but how do you want me to help?' asked Will.

Opening his Twix and passing one half to Will he replied, 'This isn't a bribe by the way Will. I appreciate you giving up your break time to come and speak to me. You are one of my best pupils; well actually you are the best by miles to be honest. Your brain works just like mine, very practical and wants to know how everything works by taking it apart. I also had a sneaky look at your school report, and saw you are also good with computers. So was wondering if you could spend your break and lunchtimes with me, working on these lesson plans. You would be an absolute life saver. I'm too old in the tooth now to start learning blimmin computers.'

And of course, Will agreed straight away. Not just because that was the type of person he was, but it would also be an absolute life saver for him too – no more run-ins with the infamous brothers. 'But I have to pop home at lunchtimes to quickly let Max, my dog, out.'

'That's no problem; I'll quickly bomb us down in the car. We can let Max out, eat our lunch on the way, and still be back in time to get some stuff sorted.'

So from that day forwards, Will and Mr Jenkins spent their break times together organising all the cupboards and transferring everything in Mr Jenkins' head into the required lesson plan format. Will of course learnt even more in the process. He saw the brothers lurking around for a few days trying to catch him but they soon moved on to some poor other person. Whilst you can't always fight someone else's battles for them, Will had no idea that Mr Jenkins had noticed too and was looking forward to them working on a new project together shortly!

After about six weeks, his classroom was completely unrecognisable and lesson plans finished. 'Thank you so much for all your help Will, shame I hadn't got you in earlier as this place is the best it's ever been, amazing! I have really enjoyed our time together too. Couldn't be cheeky could I - are you busy this weekend?'

'No, just usual stuff sir, why?' Will replied inquisitively.

'Well at home, my loft pile has just started spilling down the stairs and I could really do with a hand getting it up there. Any chance of you giving me a hand?'

'Yes of course, would it be alright to bring Max with me?'

'Definitely, I will get us all a treat in for when we have finished. Do you fancy staying for a bit of lunch?'

'Yes sir, that would be nice,' Will said, keeping everything crossed that it wasn't a ready meal. Whilst they turned out to be a great help, he really missed proper cooked food. He only treated himself to fish and chips from the chippy once a week; otherwise it was just toast, sandwiches and the good old microwave.

'Great, about 11.00am ok with you? I live at 36 Danwell Road, know where that is?'

'Yes, see you then,' Will replied.

Will and Max arrived promptly at 11.00am, opening the door to the most delicious smell. Like Mabel was here. 'Sir, that smells amazing, you a good cook then?'

'Oh just my Elsie's best beef casserole recipe, hope you like it.'

'Is she here then?' asked Will, looking around to see a chair in the lounge with a pink checked throw on it.

'Sadly my dear Elsie passed away just over a year ago, god bless her. We were together for fifty years, childhood sweethearts,' he said looking down at the floor, completely choked and eyes filled with tears.

'I'm so sorry,' said Will, putting his hand on his shoulder, and he really meant it too.

'Anyway, let's crack on with the loft or the lunch will be burnt by the time we get to it, and you must call me Alf,' Alf said smiling, quickly changing the subject. It was still too raw to talk about her without getting upset so he tried his best to keep those times for when he was on his own, often talking to her chair like she was still there.

After sorting the loft, Will sat and ate the most delicious food he had in a while, shovelling it down very quickly. 'Steady, you'll get indigestion eating that fast,' Alf said, piling some more onto Will's plate, 'pleased you like it though. I don't often bother to be honest, being just me here now.' Will knew exactly how that felt. Alf put some food down for Max, who wolfed it down and then fell asleep in front of the fire. 'Want to have a quick look at my workshop before you go?' he asked.

'Sure,' said Will, and followed him out to the bottom of the garden. 'Oh my god, look at all this stuff!' exclaimed Will, walking into tool shop and workbench heaven. Alf showed him all the things he had made and started showing him his latest project.

'Most of us in this road have lived here for donkey's years, never any problems. But you know we adjoin the estate where that delightful family were moved to. Bloody jobsworths in the council or wherever. Apparently crime figures were too high on the north estate, so what did they do about it? Put them inside and throw away the key, like they deserve? Nope, as usual, the useless idiots moved the family to the south estate, here! So no Einsteins needed to guess how things are starting to go here now. One of my neighbours keeps finding dog turds all over her front path which didn't happen before they moved in. Maybe just a coincidence, but they walk with their dog past here most days. Luckily they haven't noticed I live here yet,' said Alf, crossing his fingers.

'Doubt whether there is much you can do though is there? Will asked, glumly. 'I mean, I wouldn't approach them; they will make your life hell. It isn't worth it.'

'I know you don't want to say Will but I know they were causing you some bother. Little shites. I even spoke to the headteacher but no help there. I have been racking my brains, what's left of them anyway, to try and think of a way of catching them doing things they shouldn't be, without them knowing and have come up with this so far,' replied Alf.

Alf opened a drawer and pulled out a tiny camera lens, connected by a wire to a small cassette box. 'See this. A guy I know who works at the tip, keeps anything electrical that is thrown away for me to have first dibs. It's only going into landfill and he would prefer to see if I can make any use of it. The stuff people throw away without trying to fix it! Recently there were quite a few old cameras and camcorders dumped, so brought them back here and stripped them down for parts. What I'm thinking is, if I could discreetly setup a way of recording that people aren't aware of! Once I have got it working, I am hoping to put it outside to see what happens while we aren't watching. Good eh?!'

'That's brilliant if it works. But where are you going to put it so they can't see it?'

'Well everyone would look out for home cameras and alarms; they are always huge and very visible. And cost a bloody fortune too! But I'm thinking this could be put in a plant pot – put the cassette part in the soil and attach the small lens to the plant somehow. Fancy working on it with me to catch the little shysters, if it is them?'

'Would love to!' replied Will, with a massive smile on his face.

And every Saturday became Will and Alf's time together. Bouncing ideas off each other in the workshop followed by lunch, they both got so much from it. One Saturday, after about twenty fails, they finally got both visual and audio working. Playing back Max running around the back garden into the camcorder, and hearing them calling him, they were delighted to be ready to test it for real. Since this had all started, things had been getting worse; plants ripped out of the soil and chucked on the lawn, hanging baskets going missing, bins tipped out all over the pavement and every day more dog turds. The whole road took great pride in where they lived and their front gardens, so someone had to put a stop to it. 'Right then, let's move this into place,' said Alf, picking up the plant in its pot with the hidden camera. They nestled it in place just under the front bay window, amongst the roses. 'Maybe because of all their thorns, they have always left these so fingers crossed eh Will,' said Alf smiling, as they walked back into the house.

Three days later, Alf walked out the front door to find even more dog turds on the lawn and the bin's contents on the path. 'Right you little buggars, let's see who you are!' he muttered to himself, picking up the plant pot and taking it into the house. Digging into the soil to get the cassette, he put it straight into the camcorder and pressed play. 'Bloody knew it was you lot!' and got straight on the phone to the council. Luckily being half term he wasn't teaching, so he drove straight there to show them the footage.

'Yes I see what you mean, Mr Jenkins. It must be very annoying and inconvenient, we will send someone around to see them and put a stop to this,' said the environment officer.

'Will you let me know what happens?' asked Alf.

'Yes of course.'

Will popped in a few days later so see what had happened with the council visit, using this as an excuse to spend some time with Alf too. 'Can you bloody believe it?!' said Alf, exasperated. 'Apparently, no-one was available to go to the house, so they have just sent them a letter! I mean, how useless are these people?! Doubt whether anyone can blimmin read in that house anyway, and they won't give a monkeys about a stupid letter. The police aren't interested either, saying it's a council matter!'

'Has it stopped them doing it though?' said Will, hopefully.

'Has it heck! I bumped into one of the lads yesterday out the front unfortunately, and he asked me if I had been grassing anyone up to the council. I said I didn't know what he was talking about of course. To which he replied threateningly, *'Well it had better not be you. The council have said if we keep causing problems, we will be evicted and have to leave the area. Better not find out that it's you being a snitch!'*

'Oh god, let's forget about it then. Me and Max can pop over regularly and help clear anything up, we don't mind and better to be safe than sorry eh?'

'That is abso-bloody-lutely not going to happen. Why should they be allowed to waltz in and wreck whatever they like? They strut around like they own the bloody place. I have lived here with my dear Elsie for all these years, god bless her soul and thank god some days that she isn't here to see it. But one thing I know for sure, they aren't going to win.'

'What can you do though? I mean, the police and council aren't going to help, so don't think there is much we can do,' said Will.

'Well I've been thinking and wondering; I have a lot of time to do that now. Have you noticed how they all have the latest trainers and clothes and smoke weed most of the time, or other substances? I mean it stinks. Now unless our bloody government have gone completely bonkers, the benefits system doesn't pay enough to give you that kind of lifestyle. We know the lads nick money off the kids at school but lunch money isn't going to be that lucrative surely? I think we need to discreetly start watching what goes on at their house and see if there are any answers there. You don't have to be involved though Will, this is my battle really,' said Alf.

'Try and stop me, I could do with giving them a bit of payback too to be honest,' he said, looking slightly embarrassed.

'Three on one Will, cowards they are. You never stood a chance. Time for a bit of comeuppance me thinks, hoping of course we find something,' he said, smiling at Will.

'Just let me know when and where.'

Two nights later, 'Operation Shyster Watch' as Alf had named it had begun. This always made Will chuckle, as the way Alf said 'shyster' with such conviction was so funny. Alf had picked up Will and Max at 10.00pm and driven to a lay-by just down from the family's house. Within minutes of arriving, a couple of lads turned up at the door, went in and left again within about five minutes. This went on for the whole time they were sat there. 'Well, it doesn't take a rocket scientist to see what's going on does it. I can't imagine people popping in because of their great personalities and they leave blimmin quick too. Let's do this again for the next few nights and maybe pop by at different times in the day too, just to make sure it is daily and then we can work on getting our evidence.'

'Look, that's their dad coming out,' said Alf, as the dad came out and drove off in his black BMW. 'See, how can he afford that? Been on benefits most of his life as can't work because of a bad back, what a load of old tosh!'

The next nights were exactly the same, days too. It didn't matter what time of day, three knocks and the door opened. A couple of very early mornings, things were a little different. 'Did you see that?' whispered Will, 'They are pulling small packages out of the two small plant pots by the front door. They've just put an envelope through the letterbox too, guess that's the payment.'

'So a twenty-four hour operation without being woken up in the early hours, clever little shysters,' replied Alf. 'Well that is perfect for us too, just need to somehow get a camera setup in that large plant pot and maybe in the sofa near the front door. Let's get to work now, sooner we sort this out the better for everyone.'

Luckily in some ways, their front garden was an absolute dump. It looked like all the fly tippers in the area had chosen their lawn! Old sofas, a fridge, numerous bikes, car tyres and black bin bags were strewn everywhere, poor neighbours. Apparently they had complained to the council, but yet again no one was available to visit and the letter sent had done nothing.

So for the next couple of weeks they got to work. They spent their break times in Alf's classroom and his workshop outside of school, building another couple of recording devices to make sure they could get as much footage as possible. 'Probably only got one chance, because if they get raided or get a sniff of someone being onto them, they will move it elsewhere. These sorts always know how to play the system. It will be '*no comment*' and they'll get off on some technicality, so let's make sure the evidence is indisputable. These cassettes will record for two days, should be enough.'

As they were spending so much time in his workshop they also decided to introduce each other to their favourite music. Will's parents for his birthday had given him a '*very expensive cassette player you know, you are very lucky to have parents like us spoiling you*' he was told, whilst opening it. So they took turns between Will's cassettes and Alf's vinyl records, both laughing at some but also enjoying others. As it turned out they were great company for each other. 'Right, reckon we are finally ready now, just need to get them into place,' said Alf, picking them up and taking them inside.

The only problem now was finding a gap to put them into place, without being noticed. From watching, it seemed that the only window was between 3.45am and 4.15am so both set their alarms the next night. Leaving Max at home, as they couldn't risk him barking, Alf picked up Will and they made their way down to the lay-by. The clock ticked and at 3.30am they heard the front door being locked. Waiting and watching, two lads turned up at 3.40am, fished out their order from the two front plant pots, popped an envelope through the letterbox and were then gone. 'Quick,' said Alf, 'you put this one in the big plant pot by the front two and I will try and get this one setup in the sofa somehow,' and with no-one around, they quickly crept out of the car, leaving the doors ajar and hurried over to the house. They had practised this at Alf's so it only took them three minutes to set them up, just as someone started coming along the pavement. 'Shift,' Alf whispered anxiously, 'someone's coming!' and just as they were out the front, a lad in a hooded jacket and tracksuit bottoms came around the corner. 'You haven't seen a small black dog, have you mate?' Will asked the lad.

'No mate, nothing has passed me this way,' he replied and carried on walking quickly past the house.

'Bloody hell, that was a bit close,' said Alf as he got back in the car, his heart racing. 'I'm too old for this really, nearly given myself a blimmin heart attack!'

'We've done it now though eh. Don't you dare have a bloody heart attack on me either!' Will said, patting Alf's arm.

Two days later they were back in the lay-by at 3.30am. With both having school to fit in too, they were both yawning their heads off but hoped it would be worth it and make both of their lives better. 'Right, like before, let's shift arse,' said Alf, as they heard the front door locking again and the last lads been and gone.

Quickly digging the cassettes, wires and lenses out of the sofa and plant pot, they were back at the road just as the same lad appeared again.

'You can't still be looking for your dog? Blood mental being around here at this time of night. What you up to?' he asked, curiously.

'No, found him thanks but dropped some keys when I was looking for him. Having a bit of a panic about it, so thought would pop over now. Just found them, so that was lucky,' Alf answered hurriedly. 'Anyway could ask you the same thing, what are you doing out at this time of night?'

'Just got another phone call from the neighbours about my Gran. She's got Alzheimer's but still waiting for a place in a home so lives at home on her own. Think I will probably move in with her soon temporarily as mum is working and can't cope with it all, finds it really upsetting. Apparently, she is in the front garden completely starkers in just her hat and wellies putting in some plants, so better hurry before she gets hypothermia or done for indecent exposure!' he answered smiling and briskly walked off.

'Blimmin hell, didn't expect him to say that. Thought he might be one of their customers the way he's dressed. Teach me to be so quick to judge eh Will,' he said as they got back in the car and drove off.

After a busy day at school, Will and Alf met up to look at their work. 'Oh my god, better than expected, must have been this lots payday, look at how busy they are,' said Alf as they started viewing the footage of all the comings and goings over the two days. Both visual and audio were perfectly clear and there was definitely no disputing this evidence. Alf took copies and put the originals in his safe for safe keeping, putting the copies in the post for the police. They had already decided to anonymously send them to the police as didn't want to get involved in any subsequent legal obligations. It would always come back to you somehow otherwise, they weren't stupid. They did mention in the note that they had copies in case these tapes went missing or weren't acted on.

The following week they had heard on the grapevine about a raid in the local area, and grabbing fish and chips from the chippy, sat in Alf's lounge waiting for the local news to come on. *'Major haul of drugs and cash found in house on local council estate'* and grinning like Cheshire cats and nudging each other, they watched the whole family being handcuffed and taken away in police cars. 'Blimmin marvellous, made my year that has Will. Little shysters will hopefully get what's coming to them!' said Alf.

The brothers weren't at school the next day, much to the delight of many in Will's year. Or the next day either. The following week an announcement in assembly told them that *'due to a change in circumstances, the brothers will no longer be attending the school and are also no longer residing in the area. No further details are available at this time.'* The whole hall erupted in a cheer, with many of the teachers discreetly joining in too. The local news also confirmed that following the raid and arrests, all members of the family had been charged and were going to be receiving substantial custodial sentences in prison or youth offending institutions. The family would also be moved to another part of the country on their release. The house was now boarded up, pending the council returning it to being a normal residential home in due course. All the cash and money received from the sales of assets were being donated to a local rehabilitation centre.

Life for both Will and Alf could now return to normal. And with imminent exams and the end of school in their sights, Alf wanted to have a chat now with Will about something else that had been concerning him...

'Will, I don't mean to pry but really need to ask you something.'

'Fire away,' said Will, quickly changing his facial expression as he noticed the look on Alf's face.

'Talk to me Will about what is going on at home? Or what isn't going on, with respect to your parents. I mean, I love spending time with you and you have helped to fill in an enormous gap that Elsie has left in my life, but I am concerned that in all this time I have never once bumped into your parents,' he said looking at him.

'Alf, I don't know what to say really that won't get me into trouble. All this time I was waiting for you to say something or ask, it was just a matter of time I suppose. I think I can be really honest with you, well I hope I can. They left me to live in Australia towards the end of last year. To be honest, they have never really been in my life, it was just me and Mabel,' he said, eyes welling with tears. 'They said if I told anyone I would be put in a children's home, so have just tried to keep under everyone's radar and not be noticed.'

'Oh my dear lad,' he said, grabbing him and giving him a big hug. 'Some people don't know they are bloody born or how lucky they are. Makes me blimmin mad to be honest. Are you ok?'

'Yeah I'm ok, learnt to accept it I guess. I have had to take care of myself since I was twelve, when Mabel passed, so wasn't a huge difference to be honest,' he said looking at the floor. 'I have been able to make some positive changes to the house though, like the lounge and of course, I always have Max!' Will said smiling, as Max hearing his name came bounding up to him. 'Me and Mabel wanted a dog but were told that would never be happening whilst they lived here. So with James leaving the area and needing someone to have their dog, that bit worked out well really. Weird how things turn out sometimes eh?'

'What about grandparents or uncles and aunts?' asked Alf.

'Sadly they all passed away before I was born and both my parents are only children. I'm ok now though really, kinda got used to it. Don't worry, and having you and Max around has helped enormously.'

'Feels exactly the same for me too, Will. And of course as long as you are ok, I would never say anything to anyone, none of their business if you ask me and all I can say is you are always welcome at my door, anytime day or night.'

'Cheers Alf, means a lot,' and put his arm around his shoulder.

'Well, now that's sorted. Can you believe we only have four weeks left of school?' said Alf.

'I know, and it's just going in for exams for me now. God I hate them, but at least that's it then. My timetable is a complete nightmare!' replied Will.

'What you going to do afterwards - college?' asked Alf.

'Well mum and dad have told me in no uncertain terms that '*you must do 3 'A' levels so you can then go to university. Doesn't matter what subjects, you just need to pass them*!' he said, in his mum's tone of voice.

'And is that what you want Will?'

'Well that's what everyone in my class seems to be doing, so suppose will have to,' he replied unconvincingly.

'Blimey, with the practical talent you have for making and fixing just about anything, unless you want to be a doctor, scientist, teacher or lawyer, bloody waste of a gift if you ask me. All these kids that go to university and come out not knowing what they want to do, with a degree that is more often than not 'no use to man or beast!' If you don't want a career that requires a degree, what is the point in doing it and getting into debt?' said Alf.

'True, didn't know that there were any other options though.'

'What about an apprenticeship? You work, get trained and get paid, no brainer really. When I was younger that's what most people did, unless you really needed a degree for the profession you wanted to go into and you were incredibly clever too! Think it would be perfect for you. I have always said, everything around us breaks at some stage so you will always need someone to fix it. Everyone needs a house too. Can earn a fortune if you are good. I mean, when you think about it, what is the point in everyone having a degree? Society needs people that can do things and fix them. Having everyone walking around with bloody arts, media or marketing degrees is about as much use as a chocolate teapot!'

Will could tell Alf felt very passionate about this! 'That sounds amazing and I can't wait to be earning my own money. I'll start looking as soon as my exams are out of the way,' he replied, feeling more excited and hopeful than he had in a while.

The week after his exams had finished and school was over, Alf was on the phone and very excited too. 'Will, I have just bumped into one of my old pupils in town, who actually reminds me a bit of you. We got chatting and couldn't believe it. He now owns one of the most successful building companies in the area and wondered if I knew anyone from my classes that may be interested in an apprenticeship with them!'

'Well I hope you mentioned my name then!'

''Course I blimmin did. So I will be picking you up tomorrow morning at 8.00am, as you have an interview with him at 8.30am, ok?'

'Oh my god, that's more than ok. Cheers Alf.'

Will had been awake since 5.00am, with the nerves kicking in, so took Max out for a very early walk and was ready by 7.30am for Alf. The interview went brilliantly and they didn't stop chatting while Martin walked him back out to Alf waiting in the car. 'So pleased I bumped into you Alf, as had lost your number and the school said you had retired - wouldn't give me your contact details either. Will is exactly what I was looking for,' he said smiling, squeezing Will's shoulder. Alf beamed with delight at both of them.

Driving off, Will suddenly had a thought, 'What am I going to do about Max though? It's too far away for me to pop back at lunchtimes, maybe I need to think about getting a motorbike or something?'

'You will abso-bloody-lutely not be getting a motorbike Will, blimmin death traps they are. My brother was only seventeen when he was killed on a motorbike - have always vowed to stop anyone I care about ending up the same way. Look, things don't always work out how we plan. I mean, me and Elsie were so looking forward to having time together and freedom to have holidays when we liked, and that's not going to happen now,' he said solemnly, eyes filling up with tears. 'To be honest, I don't know what I'm going to do with all this time on my hands on my own. So no arguing, I will pop over and see Max every day, it will give my days some structure. And when you are seventeen, I'll help teach you to drive a car if you like.'

'I don't really know what to say, but thank you. Thank you for everything - I really mean it,' said Will, suddenly feeling very emotional.

Exam results day arrived and Will had done really well. He saw Alf wandering around the hall chatting to all of his pupils, delighted that they had done him proud in his final year too. As Will put the key in the front door he could hear the telephone ringing, so flew in and grabbed it before it rung off. 'Darling, we know what day it is so have stayed up especially to speak to you!' exclaimed Evelyn, excitedly. 'Come on now, don't hold us in suspense. Read out your results!' and squealed with delight, as she heard how well he had done. 'We knew it, told all our friends out here too. Said with our genes, of course you would do well!' Will cringed, imagining the awful conversations they had been having. 'So what 'A' levels have you chosen darling?'

'None as I'm going to do an apprenticeship,' replied Will smiling, waiting for her to explode.

'Sorry darling, the line's not very good. 'Applied'- what was that?' said Evelyn.

'Not applied anything mum. I've got a job with a local building company as an apprentice, they are going to teach me all the trades – I start on Monday, can't wait!' Will said, waiting for her to let rip.

'Dear god, have you lost your mind! You can't go to university with a bloody apprenticeship in trades, whatever that entails! Have you started smoking dodgy substances or drinking or something, you seem to have completely lost the plot! Get onto the college right away to get your A levels chosen and then phone me straight back!' she demanded.

'No mum, this is what I really want to do and you told me I needed to become independent, so that's exactly what I am doing!' he replied firmly.

'Well without a degree you will have a very bleak future William. You will never get the opportunities you should without it; you are a clever boy, only 'thickos' sign up for apprenticeships! I mean good god, what on earth am I going to tell my friends out here now!'

'To be honest mum I don't care and you shouldn't either. I am really excited about it and I will do really well, you'll see. If you really cared about me you would be happy for me.'

'Don't be ridiculous, of course we care about you. If we didn't we wouldn't put all that money in your account every month, for goodness sake. To be honest though William, if you are going to let us down like this, I will have no choice but to cut your monthly allowance in half. You can only continue to receive the full amount if you go to college to study for your 'A' levels.'

'Oh my god, are you trying to blackmail me?! Cut it in half then, see if I care!' he replied furiously. With that Max had managed to open the back door and began barking!

'William that had better not be a dog barking in our house!' exclaimed Evelyn, and with that Will hung up.

'Silly cow, she just doesn't care, never has! Dad doesn't either or he would stick up for me!' he said, giving Max a big fuss. 'At least you do!' he said smiling.

With that, the phone started ringing again. Grabbing it, he shouted 'Go to bed, I'm not changing my mind!'

'Will, everything alright?' It was Alf.

'Oh sorry Alf, yeah I'm fine. Mum's just been on the phone and has gone mad that I'm not doing 'A' levels. She's going to cut my allowance in half too unless I change my mind. Well I will be earning a bit to help, don't care anyway!'

'Sorry to hear that Will. You've done so well, I was phoning to see if you fancied popping out to celebrate. Grab a drink and some grub at the local pub if you like – such a lovely day, we can sit with Max in the beer garden?' asked Alf.

'I would love that, thanks,' and an hour later they were sat in the sunshine celebrating his success and Alf's retirement.

The following Monday his life took on its' new course. He instantly became part of the team and everyone took a real liking to him. On rotation, learning all the various trades, Martin also organised for him to sit his exams at college. Meanwhile Alf had become an even bigger part of his life, taking Max out in the day and regularly inviting them both over for supper. They both got so much enjoyment filling in the gaps in each other lives, like the grandparent he never had.

Celebrating Will's seventeenth birthday at the local pizza restaurant, Alf handed him an envelope. Will opened his card to see a handwritten note inside, 'This voucher is for driving lessons with Mr Alf Jenkins.'

'Oh my god, are you mad?!' exclaimed Will, 'I mean I would of course love it, and I don't have enough money any more for lessons, thank you mum and dad - NOT!'

'Couldn't think of what to get you Will, and I'm not too flush either, so thought this might be perfect! Keeps you off ever thinking about motorbikes too,' he replied, smiling.

So every Sunday at 4.00pm, Alf was out the front waiting for Will in the car. It didn't take long before he had mastered everything in the local empty car park and moved onto the roads. Whilst they had a couple of hair raising moments, Will got the hang of it pretty quickly and Alf was then able to enjoy being driven around, with a nearly normal heart rate!

By the time Will was eighteen, he was ready to take his test and coming out of the test centre, beaming holding a piece of paper, Alf sat welled up with tears.

Each pay day for the past two years, Will had tried to put away a small amount into a savings account. So getting in the car and thanking Alf, he asked 'Fancy coming to look at some cars with me?'

Within a couple of weeks, they were picking up Will's first car. 'Might look a bit of an old banger eh Alf, but it's mine and I am super chuffed! Thank you doesn't seem enough for all you have done for me!' he said, feeling so happy and a bit emotional. He drove back to Alf's house with Alf following behind in his car, just to make sure he made it ok. And as Alf parked, Will let down his window and called out 'Can you be ready for 10.00am tomorrow Alf, as me and Max fancy a day out somewhere?'

'Oh yes, anywhere in mind?' asked Alf.

'Yep, got an idea, will let you know tomorrow. See you then,' and whizzed off down the road.

All the time he had had driving lessons with Alf, he'd been thinking of what he could do for Alf that wasn't expensive but would be a nice surprise. And with a little help from Martin at work at map reading, thought he had found just the place. Looking through Alf's photo albums with him months ago, had given him the idea.

'Blimey, don't get many surprises at my age. Well not nice ones anyway!' said Alf, getting into the car the next morning. And they set off down the road, chatting away with Alf's favourite cassette playing in the background. It was only as they began reaching their destination, that Alf suddenly looked choked up and grabbed hold of Will's arm, realising where they were heading.

Alf and Elsie had spent their honeymoon here and went back for their anniversary every year after, come rain or shine – their special place. As they walked along to the bench in the photo, tears streamed down Alf's face. 'Oh Alf, I never meant to upset you, just wanted to take you somewhere special. We can go back if you like,' said Will, putting his arm around Alf's shoulders, concerned that he had made his best friend so upset.

'Oh Will, these are happy tears really. Deep down see I am just a soppy old buggar. These tears are remembering my dear lovely Elsie, who I miss every day, but also tears that you thought to do something so special. You really are someone so very special and dear to me, you know. See, told you I'm getting soppy in my old age,' he said, nudging Will's arm, smiling with tears still falling steadily.

They sat quietly together eating their fish and chips, looking out to sea. Will then took Max down onto the beach, throwing a ball for him to fetch and running with him in and out of the waves while Alf sat on their bench. Watching them down below, Alf took in a huge deep breath of the sea air patting the bench seat, imagining she was sitting there next to him. *'God I miss you more than you will ever know,'* he whispered to her, eyes filled with tears and trying desperately hard not to blink. He would never forget this day though.

A couple of weeks later, Alf got a call at home. 'Alf, it's Martin, your old pupil who took Will on. Any chance you've got a few spare hours to help me out?'

'Everything alright with Will?' replied Alf, slightly concerned.

'Oh yeah, he's doing brilliantly. Sailing through his apprenticeship and qualifications, still owe you a pint or two for putting us in touch actually. But the reason for my call today is I'm a couple of lads down in the middle of a massive barn conversion, and could really do with another pair of hands. I'd pay you of course, any chance of you helping even it's just for the mornings?' asked Martin.

'Christ, didn't think I would get asked to work again - would love to. Only thing is, I help Will out with Max his dog,' said Alf.

'No problem, bring Max too. It's only us on–site, masses of space for him to run around. What do you say?' replied Martin, hopefully.

'Fine, I can start tomorrow if you like?'

'God you're a life saver. Cheers Alf, see you at 8.00am tomorrow then if that's ok. Will can give you directions, it's not far.'

Arriving with Will and Max the following morning, as Will said it was daft to take two cars, Alf slotted into the team straight away. He absolutely thrived, feeling really useful and loving the work and banter with the lads. And life for the following few years was completely manic.

After the success of the barn conversion, they moved onto developing three outbuildings for a local farmer wanting to offer holiday accommodation.

'It's getting harder and harder in the farming world to make ends meet, so think this could really help,' he explained, showing Martin around the buildings.

And just over a year later, as Will was sitting the final exams of his apprenticeship, Martin and the team were proudly showing the farmer around for the final time. Completely blown away, they had no idea that he had invited the local press to see their handiwork, giving him a bit of advertising at the same time.

With the cows and horses peering over the fence from the adjoining fields and the ducks waddling around in the front garden and pond, they were all handed glasses of bubbly to toast their hard work while photos were taken.

It wasn't long after this that Martin was offered the chance to tender for a large council contract to convert an old disused office block into apartments. With the market beginning to slow, he was keeping everything crossed that his bid would secure it. And just as they were finishing a two-storey house extension, he got the call to say they had won the contract, which resulted in a very drunken night with the whole team at the pub.

'So have you been and had a good look around then?' asked Alf.

'Not really – mainly from the outside as the squatters have barricaded all the entrances with mattresses and stuff, so no way to get in,' replied Martin.

'God, bet it's in an awful state!' said Alf.

'Yep, I've ordered as many skips as I could. Everything just needs to be ripped out and cleared, so should be reasonably straight forward,' confirmed Martin.

But none of them imagined it would be as bad as it was. With the squatters being totally uncooperative, it took six months and a local security team with a court writ and two police officers to finally move them on. So after finishing two more garage conversions and all having a much needed holiday, they arrived to make a start.

'Crikey, it absolutely stinks - what's wrong with these people?!' exclaimed Alf, trying not to skid on the rubbish covering the floor. 'Dirty buggars!' he suddenly exclaimed, as the smell coming from his shoe could only be from a dog.

Quickly picking up an empty carrier bag from the floor, he tied it over his shoe until he could deal with it outside. 'Reckon we all need bags on our feet, don't you! There's blimmin turds everywhere!' he said sternly, scanning the room. Will couldn't stop laughing, as Alf was so cross. But they all also thought it a good idea, so started rummaging for things to put over their shoes.

That evening, sat in the pub with a beer, they all had a good laugh about the state of the place and then started drawing straws on how to divvy out the jobs.

'No blimmin way I'm going near those toilets!' announced Alf. 'There's enough shite on the floor!'

And whilst everyone burst out laughing, they all dreaded picking the wrong straw out of the tankard. Martin also had a pad and pen ready, so no-one could suddenly forget which job they had. Poor Jake.

Looking like the 'Michelin' man the next day, he wasn't taking any chances which made everyone laugh.

'Got enough on there Jake?!' chuckled Martin.

'I wouldn't laugh too much – reckon I might be off sick tomorrow and then one of you lot will have to do it!' he replied grinning.

With the skips lined up outside the parameters of the building, the next couple of months were spent hearing crashing from the rooms being emptied out of the windows and then making the place secure. Whilst a few of them had drawn short straws, they all of course chipped in and helped each other. Alf and Max though were tasked with staying outside and making the grounds secure, which both were very happy about. They were also chief drinks makers, with everyone enjoying time-out in the small portacabin for a well earned tea break.

Martin had also arranged for a local catering van to stop by at lunchtimes and provide everyone with lunch. And with the music blasting out as there was no-one nearby to bother, lots of off-tune singing helped distract from what was in front of them. Fortunately being a council contract, when the inspector turned up early on to see how things were going, he straight away offered for their environmental team to assist with some of the more disgusting clearing, which everyone hugely appreciated.

One morning, gasping for air coming out of the toilets on the second floor, Will decided that whilst Martin had recommended he carry on working in all aspects of building work to gain more experience, he might try and be busy when there was a plumbing issue. Water turned out to be such a pain (appearing from where you would least expect) and the smells, well...

Whilst the work some days was really tough going, they also had such a laugh. Max loved it, getting more fuss then ever and everyone felt like they were part of one big family, with regular meals at the pub together and supporting each other with life's ups and downs. They even turned out to be one of the best pub quiz teams in the area!

But one morning, while working on the final phase of the office conversion, Alf was really struggling. 'What the hell have I done to my shoulder?' he said, complaining of the pain. 'Was fine yesterday, had an awful nights' sleep and woke up not being able to move my right shoulder. Like it's frozen, must have slept funny on it.'

Two weeks later he was in the doctor's as it hadn't improved. He was given some cream and told to get in a hot shower every morning - that should do the trick. But it didn't improve.

Not long after, Will noticed a cut on his forehead as he got in the car. 'You ok Alf? What happened to your head?'

Brushing it with his finger, like it was nothing, Alf replied 'Oh that's nothing. Tripped over and banged my head. It's alright though, tough as old boots me.'

'That's not like you though Alf, you sure you're ok?' said Will, feeling slightly alarmed.

'Just getting older Will. Blimmin falling to bits, what with my stupid shoulder and banging my head. I don't know - I feel fine though, honest,' he said reassuringly.

Shortly after, he had fallen again this time needing five butterfly stitches in his forehead. 'Bloody annoying this is, don't even remember tripping. Weird how I banged my head without putting my hands out to save me, don't remember a thing to be honest. Maybe I need some new shoes or something! I'm ok though,' he said to a very concerned Will, and also Martin now.

'You don't have to come in. Maybe it's a bit much coming in every day,' said Martin, worrying that maybe he had put too much pressure on him.

'Honestly I am fine. Older people do trip sometimes, nothing to worry about. Probably just shuffling around not picking up my feet properly,' Alf replied smiling, 'Come on, there's work to do!' And for a few more weeks, life carried on as normal until Will's phone started ringing in the middle of the night...

'Good morning - is that Mr Will Charlick?' a voice asked on the end of the phone.

'Er yes, who is this?' asked Will, trying to focus his eyes at 4.30am.

'Hi Will, my name's Claire, I'm a nurse at Stephill General Hospital. Alf Jenkins was rushed into us at just after 1.00am. In the ambulance he was apparently calling out your name, we found your number in his wallet.'

'Oh my god, he's going to be ok isn't he?' said Will panicking, rushing up to quickly grab some clothes.

'He's really quite poorly; we are assessing him at the moment.'

'I'm on my way, where shall I go?'

'Straight to A&E and ask for Claire, say I phoned you and I will come out to get you,' she replied, by which time Will had hung up and was grabbing his car keys. Driving there, with tears streaming down his face, he said out loud 'Please Alf, if there is any way you can, please don't leave me. Or if you have to, don't go without saying goodbye.'

Arriving in A&E, they quickly called Claire who came out to meet him. Walking him along the corridor to Alf, she explained 'He has had a major stroke I'm afraid. We had a look at his medical record and could also see by his forehead, that he has had a few falls which were more than likely mini strokes. Frozen shoulder too, which are all signs. He hasn't yet regained consciousness but we are doing everything we can at the moment. Still awaiting some test results.'

Will entered the cubicle to lots of beeping machines and Alf lying completely still. He moved the chair next to his bed, sat down and took hold of his hand. Watching and waiting for any sign that Alf was in there, he couldn't stop the tears flowing. Getting up, he whispered in his ear, 'Alf, if you can hear me please can you try and squeeze my hand, you know like in the movies.' Nothing. An hour later, Claire popped her head around the curtain.

'Will, sorry but we need to take him for another scan. Why don't you grab a coffee and have five, I will come and find you when we are back.' Giving Alf a kiss on his forehead, he whispered to him 'please if you can Alf, fight this with everything you have got,' and then headed back down the corridor to the vending machine at the entrance. He found some change for a coffee and then quickly used the payphone to call Martin, leaving a message on his answer machine to let him know that he and Alf wouldn't be in as at the hospital.

An hour later, Claire came and found him to take him back to Alf. She explained that the scan was showing a bleed, so sadly at this stage they couldn't say how things may turn out. He sat holding Alf's hand and promised him, that apart from toilet and vending machine runs, he wasn't going anywhere. Suddenly the curtains pulled back and Martin appeared.

'Bloody hell Will, got your message. What's happening? Oh my god, poor Alf,' and took a seat while Will explained what he knew so far. 'Look I'll pop back later and bring you something decent to eat, well better than crisps anyway. Don't you worry about anything else. Give me your house keys and I'll go and get Max, he can stay with me for a bit. The main thing is being here for Alf,' and with that, Will's tears started flowing again.

'Cheers Martin. Don't know what I'd do without you guys.'

Handing him some tissues from the side, he said 'We're like family mate, always there for each other. That's what's most important eh! You focus on Alf, and I'll see you later,' and left to go and get Max. Will sat there thinking about this a lot. They were like his family, the one he never had but couldn't have wished for better.

Martin returned later with a bag full of food and drinks. 'You gotta keep strong for him, so this might help a bit. All the lads wanted to pop in too but said maybe when he is awake and on a ward. Any changes yet?'

'No nothing. But he is still here so that's the main thing; he hasn't got worse at least. I'm going to stay and will phone you if anything changes, is that ok?'

'Sure, of course. Like I said, Max is happy with us lot anyway. I'll pop back in tomorrow afternoon if I haven't heard from you, will bring you some more bits like a toothbrush just in case.'

'Thanks, give Max a hug from me too,' and Martin left.

Claire had handed over to Jackie at the end of her shift and she was back in the cubicle to let him know that they were moving him to a room. 'What are you thinking of doing, you must be exhausted?' she asked, starting to get things ready for the move.

'Can I stay with him in his room?'

'Yes no problem. We have a small camp bed that we could put up if you like?'

'That's ok, don't mind a chair. If you have a blanket that would be cool, if it's no bother?'

'Of course that's fine; sure we can find one for you. Ah, here is the porter now, so let's get moving.'

And Will spent the night in the darkened room, with machines bleeping. He whispered 'Night, night Alf. I'm not going anywhere, I'm here right next to you,' and fell asleep shortly after, with the blanket tucked up under his chin.

The medical staff explained that sometimes the body just takes time to cope with what has happened, that's why it shuts down to focus on repairing. They kept monitoring him and apart from being unconscious his other vital signs were ok. And two days later, he was just dozing off in the chair next to him, still holding his hand when he felt it being gently squeezed. 'Alf?' he whispered looking at his face. 'Oh Alf!' he gasped, tears instantly filling his eyes. 'Can you hear me?'

'Yep, loud and clear my dear Will,' he whispered hoarsely, as his eyes flickered open and a tear rolled down his cheek.

'Oh my god, back in a minute!' Will gasped excitedly and ran to get a nurse.

By the time he returned with a nurse, Alf lay there with his eyes fully open, looking around the room.

'Good evening Alf, my name is Jackie, how are you feeling?' she said, starting to do some more checks.

'OK I think. How long have I been here?' he asked.

'Just over three days, and do you know this dear lad hasn't left your side. Do you remember what happened?'

'Yes, I was just going up to bed when I started feeling very odd. Dizzy, excruciating pain in my head and as soon as I started to feel a bit unsteady on my feet, knew something was up. Luckily I was at the bottom of the stairs where the phone is, so remember dialling 999, said ambulance and that I was in terrible pain and now I'm here. Everything between is a blank.'

'The ambulance crew found you collapsed on the floor in the hall, with the phone hanging off the hook. Thank goodness you managed to call, that's what saved your life you know. You have had a stroke Alf but as you got to us so quickly, there appears to be very little damage done, amazing really. Definitely made of tough stuff, eh!

Anyway, that's all the basic checks done and all looking good. Fancy a cuppa and a bit of toast?'

'Would love that, thank you,' he replied, still not letting go of Will's hand. 'I knew you would be here, that was one of my last thoughts,' he said to Will, looking at him with teary eyes.

Will and Alf sat together quietly, with their tea and toast, both now taking in all that had happened.

It was only the next day when they tried to get him out of bed that he found it hard moving his right arm and leg. The doctor came around to see him and explained that whilst there wasn't any significant paralysis, his weakened limbs would require a few weeks of physiotherapy with the rehabilitation team. Suspecting this may be the case, they had already spoken to a local care home that their team works with and arranged a room for him there, when he's ready to leave.

'It's ok, he can come and stay with me for a bit. I'll look after him,' offered Will.

'That's very kind Will, but it's only for a few weeks, I'll be fine there,' replied Alf reassuringly.

Ten days later Alf pulled up outside Primrose care home in an ambulance. The minute the front door was opened, what a welcome he got.

'Good morning Alf, my name is Angie. Welcome to Primrose, we look forward to having you with us,' she said, with the kindest eyes and smile. She showed him to his room and opening the door, he arrived in his temporary home to see the most gorgeous fresh flowers on the windowsill.

'Wow, look at those, who knew I was coming?' asked Alf.

'They're from all of us here. Just a little something to say we are pleased to have you staying with us,' she replied, taking hold of his wheelchair and thanking the ambulance crew as she can take over now. 'Fancy a cuppa and slice of cake?' she asked Alf, smiling.

'That would be lovely, thank you,' he said, looking around his room thinking that he was going to like it here.

At lunchtime he sat in the main dining room and met all of the other residents. Fifteen of them in total and all seemed quite happy and content, chatting away as they tucked into their lunch. The lady sat next to him whispered, 'Always better when Angie is in charge, this is delicious isn't it?' and he had to agree.

'Isn't she the owner then?' asked Alf.

'No, she just runs one of the shifts. We love it when she is on, a nicer person you couldn't meet. I'm Sylvie by the way.'

'Oh I'm Alf. I'm here just while I recover from having a stroke, stupid arm and leg aren't working properly yet. How long have you been here then?' he asked.

'Gosh, must be just over two years now.'

'It's a lot better than I expected, was kind of dreading it to be honest. Doesn't even stink of wee!' replied Alf.

Sylvie chuckled and they carried on tucking into their lunch. Angie then came and joined them, to see how Alf was settling in. 'Everything ok there Alf, there's more too if you want it. Mind you, you might want to save some room for pud,' she said.

'Absolutely delicious thank you, proper decent home cooked food, you can't beat it. I was just saying to Sylvie how nice it is here, better than I expected.'

'Pleased to hear it, we aim to please,' she answered smiling and with a twinkle in her eyes, got up to go and get dessert.

'Oh my goodness, cherry pie and custard. If you carry on with meals like this, don't think I'll be getting better that quickly,' Alf said to Angie as she passed him his pud.

Later that afternoon the physio team arrived to start doing some exercises with him. They asked Angie to join them too. They got Alf starting to exercise his right arm first, then leg and left a schedule behind for him to follow. 'If you do these every day, your recovery will be so much quicker. You will need someone to assist you though, don't want you to have a fall whilst the strength is returning,' they explained.

'No problem - we'll help Alf get back on his feet in no time, not that I want to get rid of you of course Alf,' she said smiling at him.

'What about Maureen and the other staff when you aren't here?' they asked.

'Lots of staff changes here sadly. Maureen and Kim both left, Claire is our new manager, been here about four months now. Sharon has also recently started working on my shift, I'll go and see if I can find both of them to pop in.'

'Surprised Claire isn't here to meet us, she knew Alf was coming as the hospital agreed it with her, we need to discuss his medication needs too.'

'Oh she's probably just been caught up with something, back in a minute,' and left to track her down. Expecting them to be in the lounge with the residents, she went there first. Hearing cackling of laughter, she soon realised they were both in Claire's office. 'Hi you two, sorry to interrupt but the physio team for Alf would like to see you, asked if you can pop into his room before they have to leave.'

'Oh right, yes tell them we will be along in a minute,' said Claire, rolling her eyes at Sharon.

Claire sauntered into the room about five minutes later with Sharon closely behind, announcing that she has worked with stroke patients before so didn't see the need to attend this time.

'That's great, but everyone is different Claire as you know and we also need to discuss his medication.'

Rolling her eyes again, she got the patient care plan file out and began taking notes. As they finished discussing Alf's needs and realising that maybe she hadn't come across very professional or caring, she said smiling, 'Sorry if we got off on the wrong foot. I only got about an hour's sleep last night, lots of the residents here were up with a few problems that needed dealing with and I was covering. So I'm feeling completely shattered, with a member of staff off sick too,' and having reassured them, showed them back to reception.

'Bloody jobsworths!' she said grinning at Sharon and they went back to her office together to have another cuppa.

Angie took Alf back to the main lounge to be with the other residents. They were all sat dozing in their chairs with the TV blasting out. Turning it down, she noticed straight away that none of them had had their afternoon tea and cake. 'Back in a minute Alf,' she said, as she went to see Claire.

'Claire, Sharon, sorry to interrupt again but no-one has had their afternoon cuppa and cake yet. Can you give me a hand?'

'Oh yeah, soz, got a bit busy with some training with Sharon and whilst they all seemed happy in there, made the most of it. Can you make a start and we will be in as soon as we can? Thanks, I do appreciate all your hard work, you are a good 'un Angie,' said Claire, smiling at her and then gently closing the door again.

Luckily Shirley, the care home cook, had stayed on longer than usual unpacking a large delivery. 'Come on Ange, I'll give you a hand,' she said, and began slicing up the cake and putting out the biscuits. They wheeled the trolley into the lounge, as Angie began waking everyone up. 'Malcolm, my darling, time for a cuppa and cake,' she said, rubbing his arm gently to bring him around.

'Alright lovely, thanks' he replied, gradually opening his eyes and was then passed his tea and cake.

Alf watched as Angie and Shirley woke everyone up with such care and love, handing them their cuppa and cake, and biscuits for those that preferred that. And when everyone had finished, they tidied everything away whilst everyone voted for what programme to watch. 'Countryfile?' three hands went up, 'Songs of Praise?' two hands went up or 'Some Mothers do 'Ave 'Em?' ten hands went up, and actually they all agreed that was a good choice, so on it went. Angie and Shirley went back to the kitchen to quickly tidy everything up, to the sound of laughing which always made them smile.

Claire and Sharon quickly appeared around the corner, 'Blimey you were quick! Sorry about not getting to you two in time, cheers Shirley. Didn't realise you were still here. Really trying to get Sharon up to speed as quickly as possible, you both know how long it takes to learn everything,' and they left again giggling.

'She takes the bloody piss, she does,' said Shirley crossly, 'god I miss Maureen.'

'Me too, but still it's the residents that matter. Think people forget sometimes that this is their home, the only one they've got. They haven't got anywhere else - no choice. So the least we can do is make it the very best we can. Like if it was our mum or dad.'

'What do you make of Sharon?' asked Shirley.

'Not really sure yet, I mean it does take a while to settle in and learn how things are done, doesn't it,' replied Angie.

'Sorry to swear Ange - they might be friends, but that doesn't give them licence to take the bloody piss! Just because I am in the kitchen, don't think I don't notice what goes on around here. I'm not happy with the changes that are being made, to be honest.'

'Oh my god, don't you think about leaving as well. I really couldn't cope. With Andy being made redundant, I can't afford to think about it, not that I would though because what would the residents do without us here. They are like my extended family, I could never leave them. We rely on my money hugely now, not that it's a lot, so that's why I am doing more and more shifts. He has taken over school runs and running the house for the time being, but struggling to find a new job at the moment,' said Angie.

'Have you thought about talking to the owners of the home? What's his name, Kevin something?' suggested Shirley.

'Think that would be a crazy idea, didn't you know that she's his sister-in-law? I can't afford to lose my job. Or even if I didn't lose it, there is something about Claire that I'm really not sure about. Reminds me a bit of one of the bitches at school, think she could make my life here hellish. Don't worry, I'm sure everything will settle soon and go back to normal,' replied Angie, and left to join everyone in the lounge.

Alf of course noticed everything. Will popped in that evening to see how he was settling in. 'Gosh, lovely room Alf,' as Alf showed him his bedroom. 'Do you want to give me a quick guided tour of the home then too?' as he took hold of Alf's wheelchair. He introduced him to Sylvie and the other residents, who were all starting to make their way to their rooms for the night. Angie then bumped into them in the corridor.

'And who is this Alf?' she asked with a massive smile.

'This is Will, and Will this is Angie,' he said introducing them to each other.

'Lovely to meet you Will, and lovely that you have come to see Alf so quickly. Sadly most of our residents don't get visitors that often, maybe just birthday or Christmas, some none at all. Are you his grandson then?' she asked.

'No, we're just very close friends but he is like a grandad to me, taught me everything I know, didn't you Alf,' he said smiling and patting Alf's shoulder.

'Well, how lovely for both of you. So Alf's shown you around then?'

'Yes, it's really lovely here. You sometimes hear bad things about care homes don't you, think we've got a good one here though. I did want Alf to stay with me, but can see he will be better off recovering here with someone to care for him around the clock.'

'Oh yes, the team came today and we will have Alf back on his feet properly in no time,' she said, and wandered off to help the other residents.

'And who are the flowers from, secret admirer already?' he asked, going back into Alf's room.

'From everyone here to welcome me, how kind is that!' said Alf, and with that could suddenly hear a buzzer going off. 'They put a buzzer by our bed and also around our neck on this lanyard; just need to press it and someone will come.'

Angie rushed down the corridor to find Alan had tripped over whilst getting undressed, banging his head on the chair. She pressed the buzzer to get someone to help her lift him, as he was a big chap and no way could she do it on her own. 'Alright Alan love, don't worry. Let me have a look, just a small bump, will get an ice pack once you're up and maybe a paracetamol, expect you might get a bit of a headache bless your heart,' she said, waiting for someone to come and help. She pressed the buzzer two more times, nothing. 'Can someone help me please, Alan has fallen and I can't get him up on my own!' she called out loudly.

Alf nudged Will, 'Doesn't sound like anyone is coming, go and give her a hand Will, will you?'

Will immediately found Angie and helped Alan up. They sat him on his bed and checked him over. 'You look alright Alan,' said Will reassuringly, 'anything else I can help with?'

'You couldn't go and see if you can find either of the other two and let them know I need the accident book and an ice pack could you? Thanks Will.'

Will very quickly found both Claire and Sharon in the kitchen, sat eating the leftover sandwiches and cake from tea. 'Excuse me, Alan has fallen, Angie did press the buzzer, not sure if you heard it. She said she needs the accident book and an ice pack immediately please.'

'Oh thought he had probably just wet himself or something, often does that, that one. Alright, follow me,' said Claire, mouth full of food, getting up to waddle back to reception. 'Here,' she said, 'Can you give this to Angie and tell her I'll be along in a minute,' and went back to the kitchen.

'Thanks,' said Angie, as Will passed her the book and ice pack. After she had sorted him out and completed the paperwork, she said 'Alright Alan, nothing to worry about, these things happen my love. I know you feel a bit shaken, how about a nice cup of something and a treat. I'll see what I can find,' and left his room, beckoning Will to follow.

'Thanks again Will, all ok now so do get back to Alf before visiting hours are finished,' and she went to get Alan his cuppa.

'That girl is so lovely and hard working, they are so lucky to have her here you know,' said Alf as Will entered the room.

'I know, not sure on the other two are you? Sure you're going to be ok Alf? I have to say I wouldn't be happy for you to be here if it was just the other two. Just got an odd feeling really,' replied Will, concerned.

And with that Angie popped her head around the door. 'Sorry to interrupt, just wanted to say thanks again for your help. Alan is fine now, bless him, tucked up with a nice cup of Horlicks and a biscuit - all good,' she said smiling at them both.

'You ok too?' asked Alf.

'Oh yes, these things happen. Fine now, thanks for asking. See you tomorrow, my shift finished an hour ago so better be heading off. Kids won't go to sleep until I have read them their story,' she said smiling, but looking completely exhausted.

'Angel that one,' said Alf as he said goodbye to Will too.

Will was always going to pop in regularly but decided that maybe each day, straight from work, might be a good idea for the time being. Alf, of course, was always happy to see him and he and Angie were getting along really well too. Claire and Sharon were not so welcoming with comments like: '*you really should arrange times and days with us so we know who to expect you know,*' '*young nice looking lad like you should get a life really, instead of spending it around this old lot all the time,*' '*what does your girlfriend think about you being here every day instead of being with her?*'

Will ignored them all; just smiled at them and carried on down the corridor or into the lounge to find Alf. He knew he would never be phoning ahead to give them time to change anything.

Walking down the corridor this particular day, he bumped straight into Angie coming out of Alf's room. 'Oops sorry Will! Jeesh, can you smell that god awful stink! Poor Alf, bless him, his toilet has blocked up and the smell, well you can smell it for yourself!' she said, smiling at him and then pinching her nose. 'I've moved Alf into the lounge for now, trying to get someone out at this time is going to be difficult. This lot are so tight too, our maintenance budget is titchy – policy, ignore problem wherever possible!!'

'I'll have a look if you like. If Alf was up to it I am sure he would have sorted it, I'll go and grab some tools. The only thing is my dog Max is in the car, can I grab him some water?' said Will happily.

'Better than that, how about bringing Max in to see Alf. Bet he would love that, nice surprise as he was telling me all about him and how he used to look after him the other day. We love dogs here, well behaved ones of course. Take him straight into the lounge.'

Alf's face would have been such a lovely photo and Max was super happy to see his old friend too. 'God I've missed you Max,' he said, giving him a massive hug and ruffling his fur. 'How come you've brought him in Will?'

'Well, while you look after Max, I am going to see if I can sort out your stinking toilet. Good job I hadn't eaten yet!' he said, smiling at Alf.

'This blimmin stupid arm of mine is getting on my nerves now; if it was stronger I would have had a look myself. Thanks Will, bet Angie is chuffed too as she was starting to fret about where I could sleep tonight.'

Within an hour, the toilet was fixed and smelling sweet again. 'Blimey that was quick!' exclaimed Angie, 'Fab job, thank you. I don't have any money to pay you though and the owners will only pay invoices from the maintenance company they use. Rubbish they are too, bunch of cowboys. Usually have more problems after they have left, but again some relative of theirs. How about an IOU for a haircut? I am a fully trained hairdresser - do all the residents' hair here.'

'I don't mind helping at all, all good experience for me, especially when I am left to sort it myself. Builds up my confidence that I can fix things without the team I work with. Things seem to be slowing down a bit at work so been thinking I may have to find something else in the near future. But thinking about it, a haircut would be great as I don't get to the barbers often, cheers,' he said smiling, genuinely chuffed with himself.

On Saturday Will turned up for his haircut as arranged. 'Come into the lounge and take a seat, and hello lovely Max,' said Angie, greeting them at the front door and they found everyone in the lounge having a great time. The music was playing; some were having a little dance, some were playing card games and some were decorating cakes for lunch. A few of them sat chatting, waiting to have their haircut. 'Look everyone, Max has come to see us again!' announced Angie. Max bounded over to Alf and then began his rounds of getting as much fuss as possible. Everyone loved him, you could tell.

'No Claire or Sharon today?' asked Will, looking around the room to see that Angie was on her own.

'No both phoned in sick today. It's fine. Shirley is in the kitchen getting the lunch ready and we are all having a great time, take a seat.'

The atmosphere was amazing and Will thought if all care homes were like this, people would definitely thrive and enjoy their last years immensely. And with that, he heard 'excuse me Will, my name is Betty, would you care to dance with me?' and looked up to see a dear little face looking at him.

Instantly having a mild panic attack and blushing, 'Uh-uh-um that's really lovely Betty of you to ask me, but I can't dance.'

''Course you can, everyone can dance. Just follow me,' she replied, giving him a smile that would melt hearts and taking hold of his hands. And Will, heart racing and looking terribly embarrassed, got up and went onto the dance area. 'Go on Will!' called out Alf, chuckling.

'Oh god, this is so bad,' he whispered to Betty.

'You are absolutely fine,' she whispered back and as she guided him around, he began getting the hang of it. All the other ladies noticed how well he was doing and before he knew it, were taking turns to dance with Will. After about fifteen minutes, Angie decided to save him and called out it was his turn.

'You have made some ladies' year you know, they haven't looked this happy in a while. Handsome young man to dance with,' she said, smiling at him as she began to cut his hair.

'Thought I was going to die of embarrassment, but turned out ok I guess. They all seem really sweet and so happy here, not ungrateful and demanding like some of the stories you hear,' he replied quietly so no-one could hear.

'I always think Will that if you treat them how we would want to be treated, it goes a long way. We have to remember that this is their only home and it's not a prison. Let's make it as upbeat and fun as possible for however long they still have with us.'

'Well, they are definitely lucky to have you, aren't they? You're so thoughtful, even cutting their hair!'

'I trained as a hairdresser and it was perfect, fitting around raising the children. But then needed a secure income with my husband being made redundant and not finding work easily, this is perfect for me. I absolutely love it and still get to do my hairdressing; they love it too as having your hair done always makes you feel nice doesn't it?' Angie replied.

'Certainly does, thank you, it looks great,' he said admiring the best haircut he'd probably had in years.

A couple of days later, he walked into Alf's room to find him looking utterly miserable. 'What's up Alf? Not feeling well?' he asked.

'I'm doing all these blimmin exercises but they don't seem to be working that quickly. I can feel a slight improvement and they have said the strength is getting better, but to be honest I'm feeling a bit fed up today. I miss working and doing things for myself, going a bit doolally with the frustration,' he replied, looking down at the floor. 'Miss you too and Max. Even the lads at work.'

'We all miss you too. How about I speak to Angie and see if there is anything that needs repairing - maybe we could do it together?' said Will, trying to raise his spirits. And before waiting for the answer, went to find her. She had also noticed Alf looking a bit down today, and even the apple pie and custard hadn't helped this time. He didn't want to leave his room which wasn't like him.

'Oh my god, there are loads of things that need sorting. We have a 'maintenance and repair' file in the office that we add to when we notice problems, think I am the only one that looks at it. The owners say leave it to them to sort, but nothing gets sorted of course. Tight buggars they are, although shouldn't probably say that. You won't say anything, will you?'

''Course not. Why don't you give some of them to me and Alf to sort, he can follow me around with his wheels and help me,' answered Will, with a hopeful look on his face.

'That would be amazing. When can you start?'

'How about now - what's first?' and she took him to one of the bathrooms where the handrail for the bath was coming off the wall. 'No problem, I'll go and grab my toolbox from the car and then get Alf. Don't tell him – I'd like to surprise him, if that's ok?'

''Course,' she replied as he went off to the car.

'Any chance of giving me a hand Alf,' he said, peering around his bedroom door.

'If my bloody arm would work properly, maybe, why what's up?' he answered miserably, looking up at him.

'There's a problem in one of the bathrooms with a handrail in the bath coming off, not sure of the best way to secure it. It needs to be made rock solid so no-one slips. Could do with my best friend and workmate giving me some guidance?'

'Well I can come and have a look with you I guess,' he said getting up slowly from the bed and taking hold of his wheels.

Before long, they were working their way through the maintenance list. It was like old times. They had a look together agreeing what was next to be repaired, and if they needed any extra parts. Will then shopped for these and arrived with everything they needed. Max spent time with the residents, while Alf and Will got to work. They also became a repair shop for residents' personal items that needed fixing: watches and clocks that had stopped working or old jewellery boxes that no longer played music. They all got so much from it and Alf's mood and recovery improved too.

One Sunday, while everyone was sat having their lunch, Claire popped in to make an announcement. 'Hi everyone, just wanted to let you all know of a few changes that are going to be made. It has been decided that both myself and Sharon will be taking over the night shifts, and Melissa and Sam will be moving back to day shifts with Angie.

This will be starting next week - just wanted to let you know so there is no confusion. So you won't see me anymore in the daytime, unless there are any problems of course, but I look forward to seeing you all for bedtime. Ok?' and left the room again.

'Never bloody see her in the day anyway, lazy cow!' muttered John, and everyone giggled.

'You'll notice the difference though Angie. Melissa and Sam are lovely girls; they will definitely take some of the strain off you. We all notice how much you do, you know. We do get a bit worried that you will burn out one day if it carried on like it is now. Claire and Sharon are both so lazy, don't know how they got the job to be honest,' said Mary.

'I bloody know how! Claire is the hopeless owners' sister-in-law and Sharon is one of her best friends. Shame we don't get to vote or interview them first, especially as we're basically paying their wages,' moaned John again.

'Well, this could be for the better - hey everyone? Let's just see how it goes,' Angie replied.

And with some more help in the day, things for a short while just got better and better. A large room next to the lounge that had been filled with junk was emptied and decorated, with everyone having an input into the colour scheme etc. Will and Alf together organised the materials and redecoration. While the owners agreed with her ideas, they explained that it could only happen if there was no financial involvement from them. So Angie got in touch with some charities for help with furniture and then began contacting local groups.

Shortly after, while they were all sat in the lounge together after lunch trying to decide what to watch on the television, Angie made her own announcement. 'I just wanted to let you all know that we've got some very special visitors arriving tomorrow morning. They should be here at about 10.30am and will stay with us until lunchtime. I have organised some drinks and cakes too for when they arrive, they are really looking forward to meeting you all. I can't say any more than that,' she said beaming. And while she got the videotape ready for their afternoon film, they all began chatting excitedly about who they could possibly be.

At 10.30am the next morning they were asked to go and sit in the new room next to the lounge. They all had stickers with their names on, on their tops, and sat patiently waiting. First arrived Shirley with a trolley filled with cakes and cups of tea and squash, shortly followed by fourteen giggling little nursery children holding hands. 'Good morning children!' Angie called out, 'so lovely that you could come and visit us, we are very excited. On the trolley are plates with cakes on and two names too, yours and someone sitting here, let's see if we can find them!' And all the children quickly went to find their plate, with a little help.

'Mine says Isabel and Betty,' said a little girl, and Angie showed her to Betty. And this continued with all the children until there was one left, Sylvie and Molly.

'Oh could Molly not make it today?' Angie asked Sally the nursery teacher.

'She had a medical appointment first thing, should be here anytime now. Her mum is going to phone my mobile to meet her.' And with that, her phone started ringing. 'Back in a mo!'

All the children were happily sitting with their older person, when Molly came around the corner. She took

Molly over to the trolley and then to sit with Sylvie. Sylvie instantly picked her up and sat her on her lap, 'Lovely to meet you Molly,' she said with tears in her eyes, 'are you ok?'

'Yes, I love cake,' Molly replied, holding the plate very carefully and looking in Sylvie's eyes.

Alf was sat next to Sylvie and looked a bit concerned. 'Everything ok Sylvie?'

'Oh yes, perfect thanks. I'll tell you later,' she replied, and they all began tucking into their cakes and drinks. They then shared a lovely morning, singing songs like 'the wheels on the bus' and then doing some painting together. At lunchtime when it was time to go, Angie and Sally agreed it had been a great success for both children and residents. So they all said their goodbyes, with lots of hugs, and suddenly it was all quiet again.

'Well what can we say Angie. Thank you so much, what a fantastic morning, even if we are completely exhausted now,' said Alan, as they all took their seats at the lunch table.

'I really hoped you'd all like it. If it's ok, they're now going to spend every Tuesday morning with us.' Everyone agreed that would be great.

After lunch, the weather had brightened up so Alf asked Sylvie if she would like to take a walk in the garden. 'Love to,' she replied. After looking around at all the plants and putting out some bird seed in the feeders, they took a seat on the wooden bench.

'Now talk to me,' said Alf, 'why did you get so emotional?'

'Oh just silly daft old me really, they were happy tears though, reminded me of my past,' she said, looking into the distance.

Sylvie then began chatting about her past. She and Tom were childhood sweethearts and were married for forty nine years. They had a really happy marriage however were unable to have children, which they both found very hard. Being a primary school teacher did help a bit, being surrounded by children all day, and she eventually became a special needs teacher. Her last ten years teaching, were spent doing the very best for all those dear children who just needed a little extra special help. So when Molly, the little down syndrome girl, arrived today and was chosen to be with her, it meant so much. She knew Angie had known of her past and this had all been intentional from the start, and was really touched.

'And lucky for Molly too - seems we have both had similar pasts. I was with my Elsie for about the same time, she was my first and only girlfriend, bless her. It's so hard when they aren't here anymore isn't it,' he said, beginning to well up. 'Blimey, look at me. Getting so soppy in my old age,' he said wiping a couple of tears away. 'We both always loved children too but some things are just not supposed to be, I guess.' He then told her how after two heartbreaking miscarriages, their son George was born. They felt so blessed and relieved; couldn't have instantly loved a baby any more. But at six days old, he passed away. Apparently he had an undetected heart condition, so just fell asleep and didn't wake up. For the next couple of years they were completely broken and both agreed that they couldn't cope with any more pain, so never tried again after that.

'So how come you ended up in here, you seem very healthy and fit?' asked Alf.

'Tom and I found this place together and said that if we don't go together, and the one left behind is struggling with the loneliness, then Primrose care home would be perfect. And knowing that we chose it together, makes it feel a bit better,' she replied.

'I completely understand. If I didn't have Will in my life, it would be very empty and lonely, particularly after retiring from school. Never thought I would end up working with a great group of lads and for one of my former pupils too. That's why I get frustrated that this blimmin stroke has put a temporary stop to that. Determined to get back, mind,' said Alf, smiling at her.

They spent the next hour just chatting about anything and everything. How they both loved gardening and what they would change out here, before it started getting colder and Angie called them in. For the time they were out there, they both forgot where they were and just enjoyed each other's company. Walking back through the doors, Angie beamed with happiness at them both finding so much in common. They mentioned their ideas for the garden too.

'You two must be mind readers, you know. I was just thinking about how it would be lovely for you guys, and the children, to grow some seeds in pots and then plant them out in the garden. My local shop has got some seeds, pots and soil, was going to pop in on my next day off.'

'What a great idea, we'd love that!' they both said.

Days in the care home with Angie, Melissa and Sam working all the day shifts between them improved immensely. Whilst Angie missed the pay from working nights sometimes, she couldn't have wished for a better team. The residents were thriving from having lots of different activities going on: Mondays were for getting snacks and activities ready for the children on Tuesdays; Tuesdays were just a madhouse but a brilliant one, with them all then snoozing after lunch; Wednesdays were for gardening and flower arranging, with the flowers Angie brought in (all free from the local florist as she cut their hair in return); Thursdays were for various activities that they chose individually; every other Friday was a day for pension books and shopping. Angie arranged to drop off all their pension books with the local post office, so she was able to collect them on her way in every other Friday before her shift started, to hand out at breakfast.

Angie had found several local independent traders, selling cards, books and gifts that she setup on a shelving unit in the lounge, so they could then treat themselves or friends and family. 'Don't you worry my love, if you can't get to the shops, then I will find a way of them coming to you,' she said to Alan, when he was getting distressed about missing family birthdays.

The weekend, they all decided, was a time to relax and recoup ready for the next week, with haircuts, singing, dancing, films and tabletop activities for those that wanted it.

Shirley and Anne in the kitchen spent time with the residents too, and would try and incorporate lots of their favourite meals from the past into the meal schedules wherever possible.

Life for everyone had certainly improved in the days; nights not so much. Claire and Sharon seemed to love working their nightshifts and the increased pay, but the residents had told Angie that bedtime seemed to be getting earlier and earlier. 'Luckily we don't mind that much as generally feel quite tired from the days which we are loving, thank you Angie. But the lazy cows are even lazier, if that were possible, now they are left to their own devices at night,' said John, a few weeks later, whilst he was sat with Angie and Alf at the dining table. 'Weird though that even Alan is quiet, you know how he would always call out or you would hear the buzzer going off, nothing now.'

'Gosh, that is a bit strange. Maybe it's the change in our days eh?!' she said, looking puzzled and slightly concerned. 'Thanks for the heads up though.'

When Will turned up later to see Alf, he mentioned what John had said to Angie. 'I know you are keeping an eye on my place for me, next time you pop over I think a new plant might be a good idea for Alan's room, do you?' he said to Will, smiling and with a wink.

'Definitely, will sort tomorrow and bring back with me tomorrow night,' he said, smiling back at Alf.

Angie had always wondered how Sharon, with five kids to look after, could always work nights. There was no way she could so regularly miss the children's bedtimes with baths and stories, but at least she had Andy at home. Sharon had split up with the children's dad a while ago and apparently the new boyfriend was now taking care of them. She had heard her telling Claire how their dad kept sending solicitor letters and pleading to have custody of the children, 'No bloody way that is ever happening, I'd be skint! With the maintenance payments I get and all the benefits I can claim, I would have to be bloody mental to hand them over. I just have to cope with their nightmare sobbing when he drops them back off home, does my bloody head in. Just got my boyfriend Liam to put some locks on the outside of their bedroom doors, that does the trick! Telly up loud, grab a beer, in they go and then we get some peace and quiet.'

'What a bitch of a mother, I hope the dad is better, dear little things,' thought Angie, as she quickly moved out of

the way, so they didn't realise she could hear them. And it wasn't long before she met the dad.

'Hi, sorry to bother you but is Sharon here?' asked a kind looking gentleman, turning up in reception. It was 7.00pm, shift changeover and Sharon was just grabbing a cuppa.

'Yes, I'll go and get her. Can I say who is asking for her?' asked Angie.

'Thanks, yes tell her it's Gary,' and with that, five gorgeous children were suddenly by his side. 'Oi you lot, I said to wait in the car. Just getting your mum's key,' he said, putting his arm around their shoulders. 'Sorry about this, we have just been to the house but no-one is there and it's time for me to get the children back home. Don't want to get into trouble, you know how these things are sometimes,' he said, rolling his eyes. 'Liam should be there, but isn't.'

Angie quickly left to get Sharon. 'Well he bloody should be there, said he was going straight back after dropping me off here!' she said angrily arriving in reception.

'Sharon please don't swear in front of the children – I've asked you lots of times,' he said sighing.

'Oh shut up, bloody goody two shoes,' she replied.

In amongst this, Will and Max had just arrived to see Alf. Edging past everyone, he found Alf just coming around the corner. He had been on his exercise rounds with his wheels and was listening to what was happening, keeping just out of sight. Max bounded up to the children to introduce himself, which for a minute eased the situation.

'Sorry Claire I'm going to have to quickly pop home to sort this out, back as soon as I can. Can you hold on Angie until I get back? Liam has got the car, so I'll have to quickly walk home.'

'Yes of course, no problem,' replied Angie.

'Will can quickly drive you home, can't you Will?' Alf said suddenly appearing and volunteering him, eyes wide open and prompting him with a nudge. 'Leave Max with us, you'll be much quicker then.'

'Oh, if that's ok Will?' asked Sharon, now looking at Will.

'Fine,' he said, not really sure what was going on.

The children all looked at their dad, and grabbing hold of his legs started sobbing. 'We don't want to go home, please dad. Can't we come and live with you?' they pleaded, tears streaming down their cheeks.

'Sorry kids, you know I would love it too. But for now this is how things have to be, come on,' he told them, welling up as he ushered them back to the car.

'Oh for god's sake, stop your bloody squawking! I don't need this before I have even started work for crying out loud. Bloody whingers you have turned these kids into!' Sharon shouted at Gary and the children, stomping off in a huff to Will's car.

Will drove her home as quickly as possible. He had never really had a good feeling about her or Claire. She spoke only to give directions and within a few minutes they were at her house. Christ, what a dump! The grass was half way up the front window, with old bikes and toys strewn in it. Weeds everywhere, *'god I hope it's better inside'* thought Will, as she left to go and open the door. As Gary arrived with the children and parked up, Liam came screeching around the corner, music blasting.

'I'm only ten minutes late for god's sake! Stuart had phoned and wanted to pop over!' he shouted at Sharon who was glaring at him.

'But you knew Gary was dropping the kids back didn't you!' she shouted back.

'Trying to get me in trouble eh Gary, dobbing me in to her. Couldn't have waited, could you - prick!' he sneered at him.

'Liam, you know if I'm a minute late, I don't get to have the children the next week, sanctions or whatever they call it. So Sharon has to know that I was here on time, for me and the kids sake,' and with that, the children began getting out of the car and started clinging to his legs like their life depended on it. Bursting into tears, Rachel the oldest said 'we don't want to stay here anymore, why can't we live with dad?' All the other children nodded, tears streaming down their cheeks.

'See Liam, this is what you've caused. I shouldn't even be here!' Sharon shouted, grabbing hold of Rachel's arm and yanking her away from her dad.

'Ouch, that hurts!' Rachel cried out, as she was marched up the steps to the side door.

'Get in and stop this bloody nonsense! And that goes for all of you!' she said, glaring at the others. Gary tried to prise their fingers off his trousers.

'Come on kids, please,' and walked slowly up the steps, with them all hanging off him.

It absolutely broke him to do this every time but the legal system wouldn't help. And of course, whenever she was in court she was sweetness and light, like butter wouldn't melt. He had repeatedly asked social services to go to the house and check on them, saying he had welfare concerns. But of course, arranging the appointment, they either had suddenly had to pop out and weren't there or everyone was on their best behaviour and the house tidy. Apparently *'they couldn't just turn up, always had to give notice'* which he argued was crazy and not a true reflection on home life for the children, even their primary school had raised concerns.

As they were shoved through the door, he could smell something deeply unpleasant coming out of the house.

'What's that awful smell Sharon?' he said, looking concerned.

'How bloody rude! Just some plants and stuff that needs sorting in the house,' she replied angrily, glaring at Liam too. 'The windows were supposed to be left open, weren't they Liam!' as he walked past her into the house, and with that the door was slammed shut.

Walking back to his car, Will stuck his head out of the car window. 'Alright mate?' he said, having heard everything that was going on.

'Not really,' replied Gary, wiping his arm across his eyes. 'Twice a week I have the children and this is what happens every time. They hate going back there and have made me promise to get custody. But what can you do eh! I have tried everything, skint from all the legal bills but to no avail. Unless I can get substantive evidence that they are in danger or neglect, they have to stay with their mum and her useless waste of space boyfriend. Sorry shouldn't be offloading, don't even know you.'

'That's ok. Sorry to hear how hard things are,' replied Will, genuinely affected by hearing the children's heartbreak. 'They're lucky to have a dad though that cares so much, really hope it works out in the end for you,' and with that, Sharon stomped up to the car.

'You ready Will?' and they drove off back to the care home.

Back at the home, as Alf passed Angie on the way back to his room, he asked her to pop in. Closing the door he whispered, 'Blimey, wouldn't want her as a mum, would you? The dad looks like a nice enough chap and the kids obviously love him. Said they wanted to live with him, seems wrong that they can't choose doesn't it.' Angie went on to tell him the conversation she had heard between Sharon and Claire in confidence.

So when Will returned with Sharon, they both caught each other up with what they had heard and seen. They both agreed to keep an eye and ear out, as something really wasn't right about her.

'Ready to go and see Alan?' Alf asked Will smiling, as Will brought out the plant from his bag. 'All our modifications working ok too?'

'Yep, all good, checked it all out last night.'

Since their original designs, they had worked together on making the tape last longer and therefore able to record more footage, fitting a motion sensor so it only began recording when it sensed movement. Now it should record for up to a week before needing changing.

He knocked on Alan's door. 'Come in,' Alan called out, 'Oh hello Will, lovely to see you. How's things?' he asked.

'All good thanks Alan, you ok?'

'Not too bad, for an old fella. Bit tired nowadays but other than that, can't complain,' he replied, smiling at Will. 'What have you got there?'

'Having a bit of a sort out at home and know how you like plants. Thought you might like this in your room?'

'Well that's very kind of you, thanks Will. Yes just pop it on the windowsill over there,' he said pointing at the window.

'Evening Alan, oh Will didn't expect to see you in here. What have you got there?' asked Claire, as she arrived with a drink in hand.

'Oh hi Claire, just popped in to see if Alan wanted a plant that needed a new home, looks nice there eh!' he replied and left the room.

A few days later, Will popped into Alan's room to water the plant. 'How are you Alan? Just waiting for Alf to finish his exercise rounds so thought I'd pop in and say hello.'

'Oh yes, that's nice. Fine thanks Will, just starting to get ready for bed as usual. Feeling pretty tired to be honest, the children were with us today, had such a great time. Dear funny little things.'

'Oh that's great. Looks like your plant could do with a little bit of water, I'll just top it up from your sink if that's ok,' and quickly popped into his en-suite bathroom. He had practiced switching the tapes over quickly so not to get caught, running the tap to cover up the slight rustling noise. All done, he returned it to Alan's windowsill. 'Goodnight Alan, see you soon,' and left his room.

That evening when he got home he watched the tape. Great, everything had recorded with clear visual and audio, but couldn't see anything amiss. Sharon didn't come in and see him at all and Claire just popped in with his hot bedtime drink, returning just to make sure he had finished and then saying goodnight, turned out his light. It didn't come on again until Angie was waking him up in the morning for breakfast. Weird. *'Will wait to see what the next tape shows,*' he thought to himself, slightly puzzled. '*Maybe he is just sleeping better after all.*'

The next week's tape was exactly the same and after chatting about it with Alf, they both decided that there seemed to be little point in carrying on. Alan seemed to be happy in himself too, maybe just a little bit more sleepy than usual but everyone was getting older so maybe that's all it was – just coincidence.

Will on the other hand was having a particularly crappy week.

Mum and dad had been in touch to inform him that as he hadn't changed his mind about university, and at his age now he would be classed as a mature student and unable to get all the grants because he had left it too long to make the right decision, they were stopping his allowance completely. The household bills would be covered but he was on his own now.

Martin had called him in at work to let him know with the downturn in the market, he was very sad to say he was going to have to let him go once the apartment block was completed. He wanted to tell him now so he had the chance to find something else. If he heard of anything, he would definitely let him know and he would be getting amazing references too as had proved himself to be a very skilled and talented worker. He would be visiting Alf sometime soon to let him know that sadly there wouldn't be anything for him to return to either, even if he was up to it.

'Jesus bloody Christ! Anything else?' he shouted at the wall, after reading the letter from his parents. Max bounded up to him and gave him a massive lick. 'Thank god I have you and Alf!' he said, ruffling the fur on his head. 'Bloody godsends you both are! Right let's sell the rest of this lot,' he muttered, surveying the last of his parents furniture. It was as he was having a final sort upstairs that he found a key to a massive old cupboard in the spare bedroom. Inside was like a time warp. So much stuff from what looked like the wartime; old magazines, lamps, posters, tin boxes and even a small table and chair. Not knowing whether there was any value to any of it, he just locked it back up. The last of the furniture made enough to keep him going for a bit, popping it into his savings account as a backup if he didn't find another job quickly.

He tried not to tell Alf as he was getting so much better and didn't want it to affect his progress. Angie had chatted to them both about how he would probably be ready to go home in the next three weeks and whilst his recovery had taken a lot longer than expected, it had been a pleasure having them both around and she would miss them both immensely.

But of course Alf could tell something was up. 'You're going to have to tell me sooner or later, I know you too well Will Charlick,' he said, looking at him with solemn eyes. So Will told him about his parents' letter and then the bombshell about work. Alf sat in silence for what seemed like half an hour but then suddenly grinned, and with a twinkle in his eyes said, 'Do you reckon you could put up with me being a business partner? Even if I am an old codger now!'

'What are you talking about?' asked Will.

'Well, you have passed all your qualifications now and to be honest you are more skilled than most people I have met with twenty-five years experience. I can't leave here and just sit at home, that will send me completely nuts! So would you consider us setting up our own home maintenance business? We are both skilled and have masses of experience between us, no job too small and all that! What do you say?'

'Really? Would you want to do that? I mean, running our own business would be a dream, amazing!' exclaimed Will. 'You aren't joking are you?!'

'Abso-bloody-lutely not! I mean, look how we have worked together over the years and on everything here. It's been brilliant and the home could be our first reference of work we have completed on our own - I'm sure Angie wouldn't mind. We could take photos and list all the things we have done, just to give people an idea, and put it all in a folder. What do you say?'

'I would love it. I've got some money saved to help in the beginning,' replied Will.

'Well that's that then. I would love it too,' said Alf shaking Will's hand and then giving him a massive hug. And to help move things along, Alf spent even more of the days ahead on his wheels, strengthening his leg and arm.

A few evenings later, lying in bed thinking about ideas for the business, he just couldn't get to sleep. So deciding to make better use of the time, he got up to do another round of the home with his wheels. At about 10.30pm he was just passing reception when the phone started ringing. He left it, carrying on down the corridor but with no-one coming to answer it went back and picked it up.

'Hello,' came a distressed voice, barely able to speak for crying, 'Can I speak to my mum please?'

'Hello my love, who is this?' asked Alf.

'It's, it's Rachel. I really need to speak to my mum,' she cried down the phone.

'Alright my love, I will get her straight away. Don't worry now, hold on,' and set off to find Sharon. Going as fast as he could up and down the corridors, he found her just outside the lounge door, in the garden having a cigarette.

'Sharon, quick! It's your daughter on the phone, she's beside herself in tears,' and Sharon quickly put the cigarette out and ran to reception. Alf decided to follow.

'Rachel, whatever's the matter!' she said, hearing her daughter on the line.

'It's Liam. I can't find him! I had a really bad dream and wanted to tell someone but when I came downstairs, he isn't here. There's another man in the lounge and he won't wake up! I'm so scared mum.'

'Alright Rachel, calm now remember it was only a dream. Now the problem is Claire who I work with has had to pop out and I can't leave everyone here on their own. Liam should be home soon, is the car there?' Alf nudged Sharon's arm, mouthing 'everything alright?' She violently shook her head. 'Well Rachel he should be back soon, I'm sure he won't be long,' and even Alf could hear the crying then at the end of the phone.

'Will knows where you live. Only lives five minutes from you, I could ask him to pop over with Max if you like, just until Liam gets back?' he quietly suggested.

'That would be great, could you phone him straight away. Well once I get off the phone,' she mouthed quietly back to him, with Alf immediately nodding.

'Rachel, remember when you popped in that day with your dad and a man dropped me back home with you, he was called Will. Remember he had that lovely dog that you all liked, he is going to pop in and see you until Liam gets back or I can come home, ok?'

'Ok mum,' she said, snivelling. Alf immediately took the phone and called Will, who grabbing Max jumped in the car. He arrived to find dear Rachel sat at the side door on the steps, eyes puffed and cheeks blotchy. Max bounded over to her to give her a massive lick and she began smiling straight away.

'Rachel, I'm Will, do you remember me?'

'Yes,' she said smiling, with Max now all over her.

'Shall we go inside and you can tell me all about your dream. Let's get a drink shall we?' and she got up and walked inside, with Max closely behind. Shutting the door Will glanced around the downstairs. What a shit tip! Clothes, shoes, old boxes everywhere and there in the lounge he could see a man slumped on the sofa. The place absolutely stank too.

'I don't know him,' Rachel said pointing at him, beginning to cry again.

'Don't worry, I will sort him out in a minute. How about we go into the kitchen and get a drink eh!' he said, taking her hand and leading her into what he guessed was the kitchen although it was hard to tell. Again, mountains of crap everywhere. Putting the kettle on, he got Rachel a glass of squash, swooshed the contents covering the little table onto the floor and sat down with her. She told him all about her horrible dream and with someone to listen and Max for cuddles, calmed down and stopped crying.

'Are all your sisters and brothers fast asleep then?' he asked.

'Yes, I tried my hardest not to wake them up,' she replied.

With Liam still not back and unable to wake the guy in the lounge, who was now making some very strange noises, Will suggested to Rachel that she should take Max upstairs with her to her room, while he sorted out the man in the lounge. Rachel thought this was a great idea.

Going into the lounge, whilst the guy seemed to be breathing he couldn't be woken even when Will tipped some cold water over his head. Starting to feel a bit concerned now and seeing some paraphernalia that he was sure could only be drug related, phoned for an ambulance. They arrived and began asking questions, of which Will of course couldn't answer any of them. As they were trying to bring him around, Liam suddenly flew through the door.

'What the bloody hell is going on here!' he shouted, 'who called a fucking ambulance? Nothing wrong with Carl, he's always like this when he's had a few! And who the bloody hell are you too?!'

'Rachel had a bad dream and phoned her mum at the care home. She couldn't come so I was asked to pop over until you got back; you shouldn't bloody leave children on their own you know. And not with unconscious strangers either!'

'That bloody girl is always having bad dreams. Just an excuse to pop downstairs if you ask me, her mum is too soft! Anyway, no-one here needs any of your help, thank you. So you can all jog on now!' he said, pointing at the open front door. 'Leave!' he shouted, as no-one was moving.

Rachel and Max came down the stairs together, hearing the shouting.

'You're a bloody pain in the arse!' he pointed at Rachel, 'you know I'm never out for long. Now I am going to get it in the neck from your mother when she gets home,' as Sharon stepped into the hallway.

'Out long enough for Will to get here and me to come home though Liam. That's a bit too bloody long and you know it!' she shouted, glaring at him.

'Well if everyone is ok, we will head off now,' said the ambulance crew, making a quick exit.

Rachel started crying again and nervously twiddling her hair. 'No need for any more tears, come on now, time for bed, you've got school in the morning,' said Sharon, taking her hand. 'Say thank you and goodbye to Will and Max,' she said, leading her up the stairs to her bedroom.

'Bye,' she said, starting to sob again and giving them a little wave.

'Bye Rachel, take care,' replied Will, feeling very unhappy and concerned at what must go on at that house. He watched as Rachel was taken back to her room and as Sharon left, he noticed her bolt the lock on the outside of the door before coming downstairs. He dropped her back to the care home, both sitting in silence all the way.

'How social services visit and agree that the surroundings are a good environment to grow up in begs belief,' he thought to himself.

The next day Alf was eager to hear all about it as Sharon was very quiet when she returned. Just said, 'There's nothing really to say, all blown up over nothing really.' Will and Alf agreed that maybe Will should drive home that way every day after seeing Alf, just to see that everything really is ok.

The following day the physio team arrived and agreed Alf was ready to go home. Whilst Angie was of course happy for him, she also felt a bit sad as she had grown very fond of Alf, Will and Max. They had made such a difference to the home, not just in all the maintenance but in the general atmosphere. 'Gosh we're going to miss you Alf but so pleased you are fit and ready to go back to the outside world,' she said smiling.

'Couldn't have done it without the amazing care here,' he said taking hold of her hand. 'You are an angel you know, my love. Everyone here is truly blessed to have you looking after them and out for them too. Look at the difference since you took over the day shifts, everyone talks about it. They all feel ten years younger in themselves and their life now is filled with things to look forward to. Not just waiting for god.'

'Bless you Alf, that's a lovely thing to say. You will keep in touch won't you?'

'Of course, anything you need help with or any problems, you know you can call me or Will anytime, honestly. And of course, we were going to talk to you about the possibility of still having our haircuts by the best hairdresser around!' he said grinning at her. He had also grown very fond of Sylvie so would be using any excuse to pop in.

'That's a deal then. And we all get to see you every month then too, brilliant idea,' she said and hearing the buzzer, dashed off to find out who needed help.

Will was delighted to hear the news that evening that he was finally allowed to go home, and made Alf agree that for the first few weeks he would stay with him. They could also then start to make plans for their business.

A week later, Will arrived to pick him up. Max went to see everyone whilst they packed up all his belongings and got ready to leave. They both went into the lounge to say their goodbyes and then back to reception where Angie was waiting. Giving her a big hug and thanking her with a massive bouquet of flowers, Will handed her one of their business cards. 'What do you think?' he said showing Alf too.

'Bloody brilliant that,' said Alf. 'And there you go Angie, it's got both of our numbers on so make sure you call us if you need anything ok?!'

'Thanks you two,' she replied, and bundling Max into the car they set off for home.

'Well Will, here we go. A new chapter for both of us eh!' he said smiling at him and sticking his head out of the car window took a deep breath of fresh air. 'How about we go home via madam's house, just so I know where she lives too.'

As they went past, a large transit was parked out the front obscuring the road so Sharon and Liam didn't notice them passing. The children were giggling, zooming around the car park on their bikes and scooters whilst their parents were busy speaking to the guy at the back of the van. Opening the doors, he passed them a couple of bags of something and they passed him an envelope.

'Wonder what they are buying? Pretty sure it isn't something you could get at a supermarket!' said Alf.

'I do generally go past most days and everything from the outside seems ok, so far anyway except that night. I wouldn't trust Liam with the kids but sadly the kids don't have a choice, with Sharon working nights. He doesn't work so must be sponging off Sharon I guess. God knows what she sees in him!'

'Christ, she's no oil painting is she and even worse is her mouth. Pretty awful person, none of the residents at the home really like her or trust her, she just seems a bit of a wrong 'un. They all got together and mentioned it to Claire once but a big mistake that was. After having shouted at them, she was in a bad mood for days and everyone was sent to bed the minute Angie left at 7.00pm for the whole of the following week.'

Settling into Will's house took all of five minutes. They had a great time, cooking together in the kitchen (Will had really missed Alf's meals, the microwave had never been so busy!), having a few beers with a film in the evening and Alf had even started to learn how these blimmin controllers work so he could join Will in his gaming, that he still so enjoyed. They regularly popped over to Alf's to keep an eye on the place and also decided to keep a stock of their equipment in the car in case they ever needed it. Max's daily walks were up and down streets posting their business cards. Especially as Will had only two weeks left of work.

At the care home everyone missed them but Angie tried her to best to fill in the gaps. She setup a kitty for the residents to put whatever they could afford into and they all got quite excited deciding what to spend the money on. The last Friday of the month became fish, chips and mushy peas day, which Angie arranged with the local chippy and Shirley happily collected. She just made the pud, which again they chose, and prepped the sandwich tea as she did every day and then buttered the bread for chip butties. They all thoroughly looked forward to it, followed by a good old sing song after. The afternoon was then happily spent dozing in their chairs, tummies bursting.

Sharon and Claire on the other hand were delighted to see the back of the *'pain in the arse on wheels'* Alf. 'Bloody always coming around the corner or asking questions that one,' they agreed, and 'the only resident to refuse their hot bedtime Horlicks. So you never knew whether he was going to suddenly arrive in the lounge or kitchen because he couldn't sleep! Shame bloody goody two shoes Angie didn't want to move on as well, things would be perfect then. No questions or odd looks or funny comments.' Sharon's friend Tracey needed a job too and she would work with them brilliantly, they discussed over their evening break (which was actually most of the evening and night). Once the residents were all in bed, medication round finished, drinks made and empty cups collected, they spent their time drinking coffee, smoking fags and watching videos in the lounge. They both slept through a lot of the night too so rarely needed to go home to bed during the day. Set their alarm for 6.00am just in case they overslept.

Will and Alf spent each evening posting their business cards. Alf was under strict instructions to take it easy initially, so stayed at home in the day with Max whilst Will finished the last couple of weeks at work. They had agreed it was worth putting them through as many doors as possible to give them the best chance at building the business, particularly local houses. Everyone usually needed help with something in their household at some stage or other, and with their combined experience they could now carry out any type of maintenance and building work. They had photographed all the work done in the home and put it in a folder for potential customers to see, together with a reference from Angie and copies of all Will's qualification certificates. And it wasn't long before they reached Sharon's estate.

As they turned the corner to her house, they could see yet again the transit was parked up with the back doors open. Liam was carrying a bag into the house and came back out with an envelope. The children were playing 'it', in fits of laughter whilst running as fast as they could, when the transit doors slammed shut and drove off at speed. 'In!' shouted Liam at them, pointing at the door, and they all immediately stopped and hurried up the steps. With that the door slammed shut and there was silence, apart from the odd dog bark in the distance.

As Will got to the top step to post the card, Liam suddenly opened the door. 'What is this shit you are putting through our door?' he said aggressively, snatching the card out of his hand. 'Why do you think we would want you to do any work for us?' And he had a point, because it looked like no-one ever repaired anything.

'Um, just in the local area and putting them through everyone's doors,' Will said, taken aback by his manner at just a business card. Max suddenly spotted Rachel on the stairs and before Alf could do anything, went flying up the steps to see his friend. Rachel of course was delighted!

'Bloody hell, you can't even a control a frigging dog!' Liam shouted at them. 'Rachel, come here now and bring that bloody dog!' but of course all the other children hearing the raised voices arrived, all wanting to make a fuss of him. 'For Christ's sake you lot, go to your rooms now!' he screamed at them.

'Max come here,' called out Alf. 'You don't have to be so nasty and aggressive you know, he's only saying hello to them for goodness sake. What is your problem?'

'And who the bloody hell are you old man?! I'd shut your gob if I were you!'

Max bounded back out to Alf and Liam glaring at them both, threw their card on the ground in front of them, and closed the door.

'Good god, those poor children. What a life, no wonder they get so upset when they have to go back home,' said Alf, shaking his head.

Within two weeks of finishing at work, Will and Alf couldn't believe how quickly the phone had started ringing and the answer machine filling up with messages. Grabbing their notepad, they started phoning everyone back and arranging times to visit to see what needed doing.

'What is it with plumbing though?!' exclaimed Will, at hearing the third message about bathroom or kitchen issues, and was then smiling relieved to hear the next message was from an elderly voice asking about painting her bedroom.

Phoning everyone back and arranging to go and quote, their first week in business was already looking promising. Getting back home from their last visit, they slumped down on the sofa exhausted.

'Fancy fish and chips tonight?' asked Will.

'Sounds perfect,' replied Alf. Will prised himself off the sofa and grabbed the car keys. 'I'll drive and you can jump out if you want,' offered Alf which Will thought was a great idea, as it was never easy to find a space. And having shovelled down their fish and chips, by 10.00pm they were both ready to turn in for the night.

After fixing three bathroom toilets in two days, they were delighted to turn up to Joan's house to begin decorating her bedroom. With their overalls on and paintbrushes in hand, she handed them the paint colour she had chosen and checked whether they needed anything else.

'No, that's perfect my love,' said Alf. 'We'll shout if we need anything. Oh, actually could we get a bowl of water for our dog Max, who's in the car?'

'Oh I love dogs – can he come and spend some time with me?'

'If you're sure...' and Alf went and opened the car door.

Arriving in the hallway, Max was delighted to see Joan and frantically wagged his tail when she showed him to a bowl of water and a sneaky biscuit in the kitchen.

With everyone happy downstairs, they covered everything in dustsheets and popped the radio on. An hour later, a dear little face peered around the door to ask if they took milk and sugar in their tea. Five minutes later, she knocked to say their drinks were on a little table on the landing.

Taking a quick break, they downed tools and opened the door to find their cups of tea, a plate of biscuits and two slices of Madeira cake.

'Thank you!' they both called out down the stairs.

'Welcome!' came the reply.

Smiling at each other, they didn't really need to say anything. Their new business was turning out better than they expected.

Two days later and checking she was happy with the redecoration, she thanked them so much and was now really looking forward to sleeping in what felt like a brand new bedroom. Whilst they had redecorated, they had also helped her change the furniture around and put up some new curtains. She was so grateful and appreciative.

'You can always call us if you need help with anything,' said Alf.

'Thank you so much,' she said feeling slightly tearful, as they wouldn't accept additional payment for the extra two hours spent moving things around.

Getting in the door, the answer machine was yet again flashing with new messages. Clicking the kettle on and quickly making a cuppa, they grabbed the notepad and pen ready to note everything down. But all four messages were from the same person.

'Hi, my name is Jane and I am calling from St Agnes's Primary School. I am really hoping you can help us with some plumbing issues. Please can you call me to arrange a visit,' and she left her mobile number. The next three calls were from her sounding more and more urgent.

'Do you think it's too late to call her now?' asked Will, as it was way past the end of the school day.

'Well, her voice was sounding more and more urgent wasn't it – so think you should,' and Will phoned her, much to her relief.

Arriving at the school at 8.30am the following morning, they were greeted by a very relieved Jane Collinson.

'It's a nightmare. Our caretaker can usually cope with the basic issues but is off sick at the moment. And as you will see shortly, we seem to have a big problem in the boys' toilets.'

With the stench hitting them before they got to the corner, Will pinched his nose.

'I know – it's bad isn't it?' she said, giggling slightly at his face.

'Good grief...' exclaimed Alf, as they opened the door. The smell was overpowering. The urinals had obviously been leaking under the lino flooring for some time and the air fresheners had long given up trying to battle the odour.

A little boy suddenly flew in the door obviously desperate to go. Copying Will, he pinched his nose, giggled and said, 'It stinks doesn't it!'

'Sure does!' replied Will, grinning back at him still holding his nose.

And to give him some privacy, the three of them went back out into the corridor for some much needed fresh air.

'I haven't even shown you the toilet in the cubicle...I think it's blocked,' said Jane, trying not to giggle. But Alf, laughing at Will, set her off.

'I'm sorry, I know it's not funny really...it's just your face. Please say you can help us though. I've got new parents to show around tomorrow afternoon – don't think this will help do you?'

'Of course we will help you,' said Alf straight away, knowing that this could also lead to other work too.

Agreeing a cost, they left to go to the local plumbers merchants and were back to do the work after the school day had finished at 3.30pm.

'Bagsy you do the cubicle while I start out here!' said Will smiling.

Hearing the comments coming from the cubicle, he was pleased that he seemed to have the better deal. Within three hours, leaks were stopped and sealed, the flush was now working and toilets were unblocked. Jane popped her head around the door to see how things were going and was so pleased that everything was fixed.

'You could really do with a complete refit in here, you know. This stuff is ancient and will only hold for so long,' advised Alf.

'Yes I know. We don't have any budget for it, but I've contacted the local council and applied for some extra funding to get it sorted. As you've done such a great job, would you be able to quote for the work?'

'Yes, of course. We'll put a quote together and get it in the post to you by the end of the week, if that's ok?'

'Perfect – thank you,' and she left them measuring everything up.

Getting back to the car, Alf said grinning, 'You'll get used to it one day.'

'Never,' said Will, shaking his head.

The following weeks were much the same, with providing quotes and then having a steady stream of repairs to complete. It seemed people just wanted someone they felt they could trust not to rip them off, complete the work to the highest standard and were honest and reliable. Alf was now finding life really enjoyable. He woke up looking forward to the day ahead, usually with Max licking his face which was not always so pleasant!

As they sat at the weekend having their haircut, catching up Angie and the residents with their news and hearing what they had been up to too, they both noticed something was up with Angie. Whilst she appeared her usual happy self, there was something in her eyes telling them that maybe all was not well after all. Will and Max stayed in the lounge with everyone, whilst Alf called Angie into the kitchen. Shirley had gone home and it was all quiet. 'Everything ok Ange my love?' asked Alf, staring into her eyes.

'Yes fine,' she replied, unconvincingly.

'Really? Come on now, I can tell something is up. You can tell me you know. You know it won't go any further?' asked Alf.

'Oh Alf,' she answered, tears trickling down her cheeks and taking a seat at the little table. 'Yesterday the owner turned up and called me into the office for a chat. He had heard about the kitty, which I had talked to him about of course first and my ideas for treats or treat days, and he seemed fine with it. But apparently Claire has spoken to some of the residents about how much they put in, and he looked in the little accounts book I keep and checked the tin to find the totals don't match. I have been accused of stealing money from them. Can you believe it? Also some of Alan's pension money has gone missing too,' she said truly sobbing now. 'I only did it to benefit them, never myself of course I would never do something like that. But he said he understands from Claire and Sharon that things are difficult at home with Andy being unemployed and me having taken a drop in wages. I have had a formal warning, anything else goes missing and I will be sacked! Oh Alf I don't know what to do?!' and putting his arm around her shoulder, told her he would definitely help.

'But what can you do? There isn't anything. I haven't let the residents know as they don't need any unnecessary upset but think stopping the kitty will be for the best, for me anyway. I just can't risk it. I don't know what to do about Alan's pension. But I promise I didn't steal any money. Where it's gone I have no idea!'

'Where do you keep the kitty and their pension books?' he asked reassuringly, like he had an idea to help.

'Well, they usually keep their pensions in their rooms and the kitty is on a shelf in the office, come and see,' she said, leading him into the office to show him.

'Right then, slight change of plan,' he said, thinking on his feet. 'I've got an old small tool cabinet at home, perfect size I reckon and each resident can have their own drawer. The kitty and accounts book can live in the larger bottom drawer. There is one key to open each drawer which can be locked away in here in your key cupboard. Like you do with the medication, anyone accessing it must log it and the resident with them can sign when they take out their money. What do you think?'

'Sounds perfect,' she replied. Alf took her by the arm back into the lounge and grabbing Will, announced they would be back soon and would it be ok to leave Max with them while they popped out. There were lots of nods and murmurs of *'of course'* and rushing back home in the car with Will, got him up to speed. They quickly found the cabinet, tipped out all the old rusty contents and gave it a very quick polish to brush off the cobwebs. Within the hour they were back, with cabinet, key and a reel of white labels. Alf and Angie explained to everyone that the owner has asked that they make sure all valuables and money are kept safe and secure in the office and they just need to get a member of staff to help them access it. Very easy and better this way, and they would always sign their name in the book if they wanted to take any money or valuables out. Everyone agreed that this was probably a better idea anyway and all began trudging off to grab their pension books and money, and any valuables they also wanted locked away.

Soon there was a line outside the office, all of them finding this quite amusing and comparing what they were going to store in their drawer. Will had got to work quickly writing out the labels and decided for easiness, they would be in alphabetical order by their first name.

Angie had also already decided that these would be temporary for now as a nice activity when the children were in next, would be to make and decorate name labels together.

As Alf, Will and Max left, Angie was again taken aback by their kindness and support. At shift changeover she showed Sharon and Claire the changes that had been made, with comments like *'bloody hell, get you. It's like Fort Knox now, bit over the top though Ange isn't it'* but for Angie this was the only way of making sure she could stay. Of course, unbeknown to anyone apart from Alf, Will had also installed some additional security measures.

As they were getting in the car Alf also asked Will if they could go home via Sharon's. *'Just had a funny feeling that's all,'* he said. They turned into the estate and approaching her house could see Rachel sat on the outside steps looking really upset. Quickly parking up the road out of sight, they went to see what was wrong. As soon as they got around the corner, Max made a beeline for Rachel. That dear little girl's face immediately lit up, seeing Max bounding up to her. 'Max, Max!' she said, ruffling his fur and putting her arms around his head for a cuddle.

'You ok Rachel?' asked Will, as he caught up.

'Not really. I'm here on my own again, well apart from my brothers and sisters. I felt really thirsty and wanted a drink of water. I kept knocking on my bedroom door for Liam to come and open it, but after waiting for ages, tried the door handle and luckily he had forgotten to lock it. So I came down and got a drink, and have been looking everywhere for him but I'm scared that we are here on our own. Do you know where he is?'

'I guess then he has gone out - the idiot,' which made her giggle. 'Don't worry, we can stay with you until he gets back if you like. Have you tried phoning your dad or mum?'

'After last time, we aren't allowed to use the phone any more. Big trouble if we even touch it and they binned the bit of paper with mum and dad's numbers on so I couldn't phone them even if I wanted to,' she replied, eyes filled with tears.

'It's ok Rachel' he said, putting his arm around her. 'We're here now, look even Alf has nearly made it,' he said, as Alf arrived out of breath. Will suggested they go inside and make sure none of the others had woken up too. So they all went into the house and closed the door. The smell of weed was overpowering, good god thought Alf, and the mess too!

'I'm really hungry,' said Rachel and they all began searching the cupboards and fridge for something for her to eat. They knew Sharon was on good wages and with her benefits and maintenance payments, must have a pretty good level of income however you wouldn't have thought so looking at the house and cupboards. If you wanted alcohol, not a problem, they had what looked like their own off licence and a large cupboard filled to the brim with cigarettes, rizla papers and tobacco. Apart from that and some out of date bread, there was very little.

'What do you usually have for tea?' asked Alf.

'Nuggets and chips,' she replied. They rummaged a bit further and found some rich tea biscuits, which she happily tucked into. Looking at each other, they needed no words to know each others' thoughts.

'Think we should all be outside when Liam returns though,' said Will, as Rachel charged upstairs to grab her favourite bedtime story to read to them on the steps outside. As she was on the last page, the familiar booming music coming from a car screeching around the corner announced that Liam was back. Slamming the door as he got out of the car, with a face like thunder, he shouted 'Bloody hell. What's the matter with you two? You must be bloody paedos or something, always hanging around young children?!'

'How dare you, you little gobshite!' Alf shouted in return, which made Rachel giggle again, even though by the look on Liam's face she knew she shouldn't. 'We luckily are here to keep an eye on the children you are supposed to be looking after. What the hell do you think you are playing at?!'

'Mind your own bloody business old man. Wasn't long anyway and they were all asleep, had to get something urgently if you must know. Medication actually.'

And Alf knew there was no point in arguing and could only imagine the medication, definitely not prescribed by a GP that's for sure. 'Come on Will, let's go. See you Rachel, take care my love. Brilliant at reading you are too by the way,' he said smiling at her, and she smiled back waving goodbye, with Liam's hand giving her a small shove up the steps. As they all went their own ways Alf turned to Will, looking really concerned, 'Really think we need to keep an eye on these little ones.'

'Me too,' agreed Will.

With a really busy week, but where both of them had other things on their mind, Saturday seemed to take an age to come around. Sitting with their cups of tea and bacon sandwiches, they were deciding how to get the tape back. It was only now that Alf remembered to tell Will that he had also put one in the lounge and kitchen at the care home too. 'Bloody hell Alf, how we are going to get all three of them without being noticed?!' said Will, racking his brains to come up with an idea.

'Well, luckily it's a lovely sunny day. So how about we pop to the local bakery, grab some scones, cream and jam and surprise everyone with a cream tea in the garden. I will help Shirley with the prep in the kitchen, and then she will wheel the trolley out to the garden. You, Angie and Max can help the residents outside; meanwhile I will try and get around them all before joining you. What do you think about that then?' said Alf, looking very happy with himself.

'Do you know that sounds like a plan. So those grey cells are still bouncing around, working in there sometimes eh!' he said, nudging him smiling. And arriving an hour later at the care home, it definitely turned out to be a great idea. Everyone was so excited and Angie grabbed the CD player to setup the music. Shirley was just about to sort out their mid morning cuppa and cake, so was also delighted to have an extra pair of hands in the kitchen. By 11.00am the garden was filled with music playing, everyone happily chatting and singing to their old favourites whilst tucking into the most delicious freshly baked scones, cream and jam. Max charged about getting masses of fuss and bits of scone too. Alf on the other hand was wishing he had swapped places with Will out there, as admittedly being no spring chicken was zooming around to the three cameras, quickly putting them in his bag and panicking every two seconds that he was sure he could hear someone coming around the corner. *'Blimmin hell, my poor old ticker,'* he muttered to himself. But with all evidence removed and no-one any the wiser, he arrived in the garden pleased as punch with himself. Collapsing into the chair, he suddenly felt very relieved and only hoped that they had captured evidence that could change everything for the better.

When it was time for the residents' lunch, Will and Alf said their goodbyes and got in the car. 'Right, let's see what we've got!' said Alf.

Arriving back at home that afternoon, Will grabbed them both a cuppa while Alf got the first tape ready to watch. 'Office first then, ok?' and pressed play. And there was Angie taking Sylvie to get some of her money for a book she wanted to buy, signing the accounts book, checking her balance matched and then locking everything away. It was when the night shift arrived that things changed. At 10.30pm on the tape clock, it showed Claire and Sharon opening the accounts book. 'Go and fetch the greaseproof paper from the kitchen, Sharon. Turning out to be a nice little earner for us,' she said smirking. 'My brother-in-law says she's always been a brilliant member of staff, so was shocked to have to give her a warning about stealing their money. Just need to keep making these changes and she'll be out of here.'

'I mean they'd give us a tip if we were in a restaurant looking after them, serving them and making sure they were ok. Don't feel any guilt, I mean how much more stuff can they want to buy when they are going to be kicking the bucket soon anyway, waste of money if you ask me,' Sharon said sniggering.

With all the residents fast asleep, they spent the next hour making adjustments to the book and taking out money from each resident's pension, just small amounts and of course under Angie's signature that had been carefully traced. Gloating over how much it came to, they hid the money in Claire's locker. They repeated this again later on in the week too.

Will and Alf just sat in silence, taking it all in. 'What bitches,' said Alf, 'always knew there was something wrong with those two. Got the feeling they didn't like me either. Always 'tutting' as I came around the corner in the evenings when I couldn't sleep. Would never help me with my exercises either. I'm really looking forward to seeing what they get up to on the other tapes too.'

Next was the kitchen tape. Shirley busy throughout the day singing along to the radio, with Angie and Sam popping in and out too. A moment of silence, then Claire can be heard saying goodbye to Angie and then entering, putting the kettle on. Sharon popping her head around the door, 'give us a shout when you are ready' and then lining up all the cups. Horlicks in, milk and then hot water. Stir, crumble up tablet and sprinkle, stir, ready. 'What the hell is that?' exclaimed Alf. Reaching into her pocket, she then took out another bottle and put them on the side - sleeping tablets. 'Bloody knew Alan wasn't just settling. Knew it was weird how everyone put it down to his busy days as to the reason for him sleeping so much better.' And they watched her add it to many of the other cups too.

Sharon appeared again, with Claire pointing out the ones for Alan and the others with their 'special ingredient' in and she was careful to put them on the trolley in the correct order. 'Important we know whose is whose, at least we don't have to worry about bloody Alf suddenly appearing from nowhere now, like he is keeping an eye on us, bloody pain in the arse old git,' she said, smiling at Sharon. Half an hour later, they returned to the kitchen, all cups empty and quickly washed away any evidence. Cups returned to cupboard, lights out and silence again. The next nights were all the same too.

Alf sat shaking his head whilst he put in the last tape. Lounge by day was filled with laughter, haircuts, activities, the children arriving, looking at the new things to buy that had arrived, singing, watching films. By night when Claire and Sharon were on shift, couldn't be more different. Door opening, giggling that everyone was fast asleep and guaranteed wouldn't be disturbed, glass of wine, crisps and cake, watch TV or a film and few hours sleep on the sofas. Set alarm for 6.00am, so all evidence hidden away again and residents being woken up with a cup of tea, all sweetness and light. 'Morning - had a good sleep?' and then quick handover with the day team before leaving. Every night was the same.

'Unbelievable! And they get paid for that!' said Alf angrily. 'Sister-in-law or not, the owner has to act on seeing all of this. Tell you what, whilst it will be sent to him anonymously, the note will also say that the council will also be getting a copy, so he had better act on it quick too!'

Alf launched himself out of his chair so fast, he nearly took a tumble. 'Careful Alf, honestly don't get so stressed, we don't want you having another stroke. Let's just be thankful that we have all of this and get it posted quickly. Tell you what - let's grab some fish and chips for tea before our walk with Max. Get those tapes copied and then let's hand deliver the evidence today. I know where the owner lives as had to drop something off at his house once, as a favour for Angie, and the council offices are close to one of the best chippies around.'

Alf quickly began duplicating and labelling the tapes, keeping the original for themselves of course, just in case these things happened to go missing. By 6.00pm they were in the car posting the evidence. They quickly shovelled down their fish and chips, and then parking back at home grabbed Max ready for his walk. 'Blimey, this stress is causing havoc with my insides Will, I am so mad with them you know!'

'I know. But let's park it for now and check on these children eh?' said Will.

'Let's hope things are better there today. Should be, as Sharon isn't working tonight,' replied Alf.

They both walked towards the estate in silence, still trying to process the care home tapes, that had more concerning footage than either of them would have imagined. Turning the corner, Max suddenly spotted a squirrel and started chasing it, pulling Will along with him. They ended up running right up to the car park outside Sharon's house, where there were some large trees. Whilst the squirrel easily outran Max, he didn't give up and was very happy to be distracted by the children arriving at the trees. 'Max, lovely Max!' they called out, running up to him and giving him a big cuddle.

'Hi Rachel and all of you. What are you all up to then?' asked Will, looking around and half expecting dimwit Liam to come flying out of the door.

'Oh, just playing out. Not our bedtime yet,' replied Rachel.

'That's nice. Max hasn't been on a big walk this week as we've been so busy. So how nice for us to bump into you all too,' he said, as some cuddled Max whilst the others started kicking a football towards him for a game. Alf then arrived, having finally caught up.

'Blimey that dog is fast! Hi kids!' he called out.

'Oh hi, do you want to join in our game of football?' asked Louis.

'That would be fun, what about your mum and her boyfriend?' asked Alf, seeing that the car was there.

'They're just having a sleep at the moment, so that's why we are playing outside - so we don't wake them up,' replied Rachel.

'Oh right. Would love to, wouldn't we Will. Only problem is I am absolutely busting for a wee, couldn't quickly use your toilet could I?' asked Alf.

''Course you can. Louis and Will setup the goals and I'll show Alf where the toilet is,' said Rachel skipping along. Showing him into the house and pointing up the stairs, she whispered, 'Second door on the right ok. Quiet though so they don't wake up,' and he could see Sharon and Liam both completely 'sparko' in the lounge. She ran back outside while Alf pretended to go up the stairs. Once she had gone, he crept into the lounge to find tobacco, little bags of green leaves, empty bottles of wine and vodka and two adults completely out of it. He went back outside to join the football game, shaking his head. Once they were all tired out and Max had even collapsed on the floor after joining in, much to the delight of the children who had spent the whole time giggling and laughing, it was time for them to go.

'Rachel, why don't you go and ask your mum if it's your bedtime yet, love?' said Alf.

'Ok,' and she ran in. She came back out quite quickly concerned that mum wouldn't wake up.

'Let me have a go,' said Alf and went in to give them both a firm shake. Nothing.

Going back outside, he asked what her dad's name was. As she answered, he went back in the house, extracted one of their phone books and quickly flicked through to find his number. Knowing that no-one was about to wake up anytime soon, he phoned and spoke to Gary, relaying his concerns. Ten minutes later, the children squealed with delight as their dad's car came around the corner. Parking up, he opened the door to five children all grabbing at his arms and legs, 'Dad, what are you doing here?' they all asked, clinging onto him.

'Just thought I would pop over and say hello, that's all. Missing you all,' he replied, cuddling them and smiling. 'What are you doing out now anyway? It's getting late, nearly bedtime and you are all out here not even in your pyjamas yet?'

'Oh we've just been playing football with Will, Alf and Max. Having a great time dad,' replied Rachel.

'Well, that's great but I think it must be time to be calming down a bit now too. PJs, drink and a story I reckon would be a good idea, where's your mum?' he asked, knowing the answer from his phone conversation with Alf.

'She's already asleep - Liam is too,' and Gary walked as calmly as possible, up the steps into the lounge. Seeing the state of the place and those two, he quietly asked the children to grab anything they wanted to take with them as they were going to his place for the night.

Thanking Alf and Will, Gary whispered 'See, how can it be better for them to live here? Bloody crazy, I worry all the time you know,' and jumped in the car with five very excited children. Putting Max back on his lead, they looked back to see the door wide open, children gone and no-one any the wiser.

Shaking his head again and looking at Will with eyes filled with tears, Alf said 'Those poor little beggars. These jobsworth social workers should be ashamed of themselves leaving them there, how can anyone not see that they would be better off with their dad? Begs belief doesn't it? Hang on a sec - I'm just going to make a quick call to the police to report a concern for welfare. Let's see what they think about it,' as he quickly shot into the phone box.

Fifteen minutes later, a police car was drawing up outside Sharon's house following an anonymous call.

Knocking on the open door and calling out hello, there was no answer. Peering in, he then called out their names, still no answer. Walking into the lounge he could see them both unconscious on the sofa and quickly checked for breathing and pulse. All fine there, so started looking around. Seeing the glass coffee table covered with drugs paraphernalia, he quickly made a call. Within ten minutes, and with neither of them even stirring, the drugs unit arrived. Packing up all the evidence on the table, they started looking around the house. Inside the kitchen and lounge, they found two locked cupboards. 'Going to need a warrant to look in here,' one of them said, 'let's get back to the station with what we have so far, get the warrant and then get these padlocks off,' and with that, they all left the house, closing the door. No need for an ambulance was recorded - *'will just leave them to sleep it off,'* concern that children live here was also noted, contact social services urgently.

Hearing something come through the letterbox, the care home owner was shortly watching the footage, devastated and completely dumbfounded. 'How could they do this, family or not, I completely trusted her to run it for me?

Should have been more involved and made more checks,' he said to himself, shaking his head.

By 9.00am the following morning, it was no surprise that social services were on the phone to him explaining that they would be meeting him at the care home with the police shortly. The council would be taking back ownership of the care home and day to day running for now, until they found someone else. They would also be visiting Claire and Sharon at their homes. They also told him another team would be also be visiting Sharon on another matter, although couldn't say any more. Questioning her suitability to work in this environment, they asked what references they had received for her. Arriving and checking her personnel file, he could see that no references had been received, *'for god's sake Claire, you know no-one should start work without them,'* he muttered to himself.

Whilst Claire's day was about to take a big downward turn with an imminent arrest, Sharon had no idea what was on her horizon in the next hour. She and Liam were woken up by loud hammering on the door. 'What the bloody hell?!' shouted Liam angrily and got up to answer it. Opening the door, a police team together with the family social worker were stood there waiting. Showing the warrant, they pushed their way into the lounge.

'What bloody busybody has called the bloody rozzers?!' Sharon shouted at them. 'You can see we are fine!' and then looked down to see the scribbled note from Gary, that as he couldn't wake them, had taken the children back to his.

'He's taken the children!' she screamed at the policeman. 'Don't bloody stand there staring at me! Go and get my kids!' He just looked at her and said nothing. Liam was now standing in the way of the cupboard, telling them in no uncertain terms that they were not going to be opening it. Showing the warrant, they forcefully moved him out of the way and smashed the locks off. Both cupboards were filled to the brim with drugs, scales, cling film, bags and cash. The policeman just looked at both of them and calmly explained that they were both going to be arrested and read them their rights. Expecting Liam to become violent, three officers quickly piled on top of him and put on the handcuffs, Sharon was luckily more placid. The social worker had then taken a further look around the house and the virtually empty cupboards and fridge in the kitchen. Shaking her head and looking very solemn, she apologised to the children quietly to herself. She knew this was partly her fault.

She just looked at Sharon, shaking her head and went back out to her car.

With all the children sat at the table tucking into their breakfast, Gary looked at his phone ringing, dreading the call he was about to take. He knew it hadn't been his day to have the children, but 'for god's sake' he couldn't have left them. Taking a deep breath, he knew Jan, their social worker, was likely to be telling him that access arrangements were going to be reduced again for non-compliance. 'Hello Jan,' he answered nervously. And as she began to explain everything that had happened over the past eighteen hours, the world instantly got a lot brighter. 'Right ok, no that's fine. I'll be over with the children in about thirty minutes if that's ok. Just need to quickly get them dressed as they are still in their pyjamas eating their breakfast. Thank you Jan, thank you,' and put the phone down on the table.

'Who was it dad?' asked Rachel.

'Kids, that was Jan, you know the lady that visits sometimes to see you are ok. She has just been to the house and your mum and Liam have been naughty and are in trouble for not looking after you very well. She has decided that it would be better if you came and lived with me now, everyone ok with that?!' he said, with tears streaming down his cheeks.

'Yey!!!' Everyone danced around, laughing and giving each other massive cuddles.

'Forever?!' Louis suddenly stopped and asked hesitantly.

'Yes, forever and ever! So we need to quickly get dressed and go over to your house. Jan is waiting to meet us there so you can pick up anything you want, as you won't be going back there again.' The children flew up the stairs so fast and arrived back down in very odd attire, they had obviously grabbed the first things they came to. Laughing, Gary bundled them all into the car and headed for the house.

Meanwhile Alf and Will had also woken up early and were both desperate to know what might be happening. Deciding Max needed another walk, they set off to see if anything was going on at the house.

A white transit van began making its way down the road and seeing all the commotion going on outside the house, quickly carried on down the road. *'Shit'* was muttered from inside as they were now going to have to find someone and somewhere else.

'Blimmin hell, result!' exclaimed Alf quietly, as they turned into the road. Three police cars, a police van and a lady sat in an estate car. They watched from a distance as Liam and Sharon were shown into the police van and quickly driven off. 'Looks like it worked Will,' he whispered. Another car then turned up as the other police cars started leaving.

They both smiled at each other as they neared, with Max going for a wee up against the tree. As soon as the car had parked, the doors opened and five children rushed out. Louis spotted Max, and flew over to say hello whilst the lady sat in the estate car, got out and walked up to Gary. Spotting Louis with Max, the others went to say hello too, whilst Gary began chatting with the lady.

'You all ok?' asked Alf.

'Absolutely brilliant actually!' exclaimed Rachel. 'You won't believe it. Daddy got a phone call this morning from that lady and because mum and Liam aren't very good at looking after us, she has decided that we should live with Dad, can you believe it?!'

'Well, that does sound brilliant!' said Will smiling.

'We're just here to pick up any stuff we might want to keep, as we won't be coming back again. So better hurry, come on everyone!' and she ushered her brothers and sisters towards the house.

Gary soon joined them in the house with Jan, and they watched as each child ran into the bedroom grabbing the odd blanket and teddy that meant something to them. There wasn't much to take anyway, as most of the rooms were bare apart from things that shouldn't be in there anyway.

As they began to walk off, Gary and the children called out to them. 'Bye, thank you!'

Gary was so relieved that it was finally all over. It was just him and the kids now - how it should always have been.

The house was emptied and boarded up by the council until it could be renovated.

Later that day they turned up at the care home to see if anything had changed their too. Whilst the children were their number one priority, Angie wasn't far behind.

Walking into reception, they bumped straight into Angie who asked them to follow her into the kitchen.

'You won't believe it! Come on, grab a seat while I make us a cuppa and tell you my news! What a crazy day. The minute I got in, the owner was waiting for me and asked me to go into the office. Obviously after our last meeting, I was a nervous wreck wondering what on earth I had done now. Well, what does he want to do? He wants to apologise! Apparently he had discovered, not sure how, that Claire and Sharon were pulling a fast one here, taking the piss work wise but also been withdrawing funds that were not theirs, I think that's how he put it anyway. He was concerned about levels of care they were providing, or not as was the case. He also wanted to thank me for all I had done here and what an amazing, caring person I was. Reluctantly he will no longer own and be in charge of the overall running of the care home and then said someone from the council will be arriving at 10.30am to meet me!'

Taking a massive breath and a glug of tea, she continued, 'Maggie arrived dead on 10.30am to let me know that she would be my contact for now, until someone takes on ownership of the home. Apparently Claire and Sharon have both been sacked! Then you won't believe this bit either, she is so impressed with me, although not sure what she knows, that I have been promoted to manager with a large salary increase to go with it. I mean, it must nearly be classed as a miracle! My prayers have been answered, can you believe it?! She has even given me a bonus of five hundred pounds!'

'Well all I can say is that it's well deserved my love,' said Alf.

'That's not all. She has also asked me to find a local company to help with all the ongoing repairs and maintenance. She suggested three mornings a week, if I knew of anyone. And telling her all about you two and showing her what you had done so far, she said to get in touch with you straight away!'

'Oh wow, that's brilliant! Of course we would love to help and work for you - that's amazing! replied Will.

'Do the residents know about the changes yet?' asked Alf.

'Not yet, it's been completely manic this morning so thought I would let them know at lunch,' Angie replied, feeling the happiest she had felt in a while. Only now did she realise how massive the cloud that had been hanging over her was since the theft accusation, and the sudden feeling of relief was nearly overwhelming. 'Do you know I think everything is going to be ok now. Let's just hope the new owner turns out better than the last one at recruitment eh!' and with a buzzer being pressed, set off to see what the problem was.

Of course on hearing the news, the lunch table turned into a massive celebration with lots of clapping and hugs all around. Within two weeks, being tasked with replacing Claire and Sharon and an extra pair of hands too, Angie had recruited three new members of staff and was beginning their training. Andy and the girls were so proud of her and the increase in pay made life at home so much easier. No more panicking when the post arrived, with arrears bills in bold red landing on the floor.

Eight weeks later Maggie phoned to say they had found a new owner who wanted to meet her and have a look around the home before signing on the dotted line. Feeling terribly nervous before his arrival, Angie had hardly slept. When Simon arrived, all her worries were dispelled within five minutes. The most charming, kind person she was to meet for some time, who ran one other care home about an hour's drive from here. She could instantly tell it was for his passion (not the income) that he had chosen this career. After looking around, asking lots of questions and beaming at all the answers, he asked to sit with everyone for lunch. He found out about all the residents while they tucked into their lunch together, laughing and joking with them and hearing all about the wonderful ideas Angie had put into place over their week. From the children to gardening, dancing, games, haircuts, quizzes, beetle drives, shopping and films, he knew that it would be a privilege to be a part of their lives.

Saying goodbye to everyone and thanking the rest of the staff for their time, he walked with Angie back out to reception. 'Well I can honestly say that I have enjoyed spending this time with you all so much and you are completely fantastic. Just hope you know that. It would be an honour and privilege to take over the ownership of this home, as long as you stay of course,' he said, smiling at her.

'Gosh, I am completely taken aback, thank you. Oh yes, I can never see myself leaving,' she replied smiling, quite overwhelmed with the compliments.

'Well that's done then. I'll be in touch with Maggie and will come back and visit you all soon when everything has gone through. Maybe we could organise a party or something for everyone?'

'They would love that, yes - just let me know, and with Shirley's help in the kitchen we will sort something out. If it's a Tuesday you can meet the children too.'

'I would love that, thank you,' Simon replied and left to return to his other home.

Now Simon's other care home was different to Primrose. Green Meadows was a care home who also provided care for slightly more challenging residents. Just over half the residents had dementia or Alzheimer's which certainly made daily life there interesting. Security to ensure they were kept safe and 'no escapees' was a priority as well as adapting things to help them. He thought it would be interesting though to see if any of Angie's ideas could work for them too, with maybe just a bit more assistance.

Angie was invited to visit his other care home the following week. A taxi turned up to collect her and she was whisked away into the countryside. Arriving at the home, she marvelled at the beautiful rural surroundings. If anyone did escape, it would only be to fields for the first mile but she guessed this could possibly make it even harder to find them. Simon clicked open the door with the pass on his lanyard and greeted her with open arms. Thanking her for coming up, she was soon introduced to some of the residents. 'Is it time for the bus yet?' asked a lady rushing up to them, 'I hope I haven't missed it again,' she said glumly sighing.

'No, you're just fine Agnes. Take a seat and I will go and find Alison,' Simon replied, showing her to the plastic chair in the hall by the stairs.

'That one is completely barking you know!' said a gentleman, shuffling his way towards them.

'Morning Bert, how are you this morning?' Simon asked him smiling.

'Oh same old, same old - mustn't complain really. Come on Agnes, the bus is going to be ages yet, let's go in the lounge for a cup of tea,' he said smiling at Agnes, and taking her by the arm led her off down the hall to the lounge.

'Smashing chap he is, really funny too. So sad that he lost his wife about a year ago and really struggling with the isolation came for a visit, just to have a look around. Moved in the next week and has been so much happier since. Loves helping too if he can. Pleasure to have him here,' he said, whilst starting to show Angie around.

Whilst the home atmosphere was really lovely, it was really quite scruffy too, Angie thought. Simon must have been reading her thoughts because at the end of the tour he asked if she knew anyone trustworthy and reliable to help with repairs and maintenance. She explained all about how Alf and Will had completely transformed Primrose, and all really to aid Alf's recovery and they had continued to be a very important part of their care home. 'Not sure how it would work though as they have already agreed to three mornings a week working with us. I could see if they could recommend anyone though?' she offered.

'That would be great. Trying to find anyone trustworthy and who gets on with the residents is nearly impossible - and as you can see, a lot needs doing here.'

Chatting with Alf and Will about the new owner and the other home, she then mentioned the tattiness of the interior and the conversation with Simon. 'Know anyone?' she asked.

'Well, I know everything here is pretty much ok now, just odd leaks and repairs that need sorting when they happen. I like doing some woodwork with the residents on their activity days, so the only thing we could maybe consider is if Will went up and stayed there for a few weeks when our current jobs are finished. Only of course if that's ok with you Will?' suggested Alf.

'Yes I'd be fine with that. If they could sort out some accommodation for me to save all the wasted time travelling and costs too, I would definitely be happy to help. How about you give me Simon's number and I'll arrange a visit, to see exactly what needs doing. Alf can come with me and we can then come up with a plan for me to follow and also confirm costs involved,' replied Will.

'Brilliant, you'll really like him,' she said smiling at them, digging through the drawer for a pen and paper to write down his number.

Cracking on with all their current jobs, they squeezed in a morning visit to Green Meadows. Driving through the nearby village, they arrived up the gravel drive to the most stunning looking home set in its' own grounds. Parking up, Simon warmly greeted them, thanking them so much for taking the time to come and see the home. Good god, it needed a lot of work but nothing that would be too much of a problem. Mainly decorating, patch repairs and also sorting out some issues with plumbing and drains, from the smell that was coming out of a disused room by the kitchen. A couple of the residents also introduced themselves, one of them thinking Will was her son coming to visit her. Seeing how Will was so caring in his response, Simon just prayed and hoped he would say yes, which of course he did.

One afternoon shortly after, they got a call from a very excited customer.

'Hi Will – it's Jane from St Agnes's Primary School. Great news - I got the funding at last! And based on the quotes and testimonials we received, the governors have agreed to give the contract to you! Isn't that great?!'

'Absolutely! Thank you,' replied Will. 'Any idea when you are looking at it being done?'

'I was really hoping for four weeks time – during our half term break, if you can manage that?'

'The only thing is, as it's been a while, things have changed slightly here. I'm going to be working away for a few weeks so we weren't planning on taking on any new work until I get back.' But hearing the disappointed sigh, he suddenly said, 'Actually I'm sure we can still help. Let me give an ex-colleague a quick call and see if he is available to work with Alf. I'll call you straight back.'

Twenty minutes later, having got hold of Jake, he was on the phone to Jane again. 'All sorted. Jake will do the refit with Alf, is it ok I bring him over to meet you and show him what needs doing?'

'Um, er, I guess. Is he good though?' she answered hesitantly.

'Yes - we all worked together for years. I can assure you he and Alf will do a brilliant job.'

'OK. Can you pop over at the end of the school day on Friday then – say 3.45pm?'

'Perfect – we look forward to seeing you then.'

Alf was just coming down the hallway at the end of the conversation. 'Who was that then?'

'Jane from St Agnes's about the toilet refurbishment. We got the contract Alf – isn't that great? I gave Jake a quick call as she really wants us to do it during their half term in four weeks, while I will be away, and he would love to work with you on it.,' he said grinning.

'Hope he's still got that Michelin man outfit and maybe a spare for me!' said Alf chuckling.

On Friday, dead on 3.45pm, the three of them were stood in reception waiting for Jane.
Breezing down the corridor and scanning her lanyard to unlock the door, she welcomed them back.
'Jane this is Jake,' Will introduced them.
'Nice to meet you Jake and we so look forward to our loos being finally sorted.'
Turning the corridor, Jake instantly sniffed and looked at them both.
Leaving the school, having confirmed the work to be done and timings, they headed back to the car.
'Jesus Christ – it might be as bad as the office block we did!' exclaimed Jake. 'Might try and find some gas masks for me and you, Alf!'

A month later, Alf and Jake were heading for St Agnes's school toilet block while Will made his way up to Green Meadows. Simon had sent him details of where he would be staying and Will headed straight for Willows bed and breakfast, to check in, dump his luggage and take a short walk up the hill to the home. The owner was so welcoming and with nothing too much trouble, he was quickly shown his room and around the house, before he left to start work.
Simon introduced him to the other carers and whilst they walked around the home, agreeing colour schemes etc and ordering the work, Will felt so content and happy - he just got that really good feeling that so rarely happens in our lives. Like you are supposed to be somewhere...

After lunch, Will walked back down the hill to go and get the paint from the local hardware store in the village where Simon had setup an account, *'yes the big superstores might be a bit cheaper, but it is more important that we all support each other locally, especially in this village'* Simon explained. Very handy for Will to pop in and, as is often the case, the friendliness and helpfulness of the three people working there made Will wish he had something like this local to him back home.

The next day he arrived and started cracking on with stripping off the most gopping wallpaper he had probably ever seen. 'This should really come with a health warning, it's so bad for the eyes!' he joked with Bert, as he came to see what was going on. Bert chuckled in agreement.

'Is it ok if I come and watch?' he asked Will.

'Of course you can. Unless you are supposed to be somewhere else and I will get into trouble,' Will replied smiling at him.

'Oh no, it's very relaxed here, it really is like being in your own home just with lots of people for company and help if you need it. Lovely meals too and no cleaning, so what's not to like eh! I even get to have a couple of pints on a Friday and Saturday night like I used to and even my favourite pork scratchings,' Bert replied, looking thoroughly content with the world.

And while Will battled with the wallpaper that decided it was actually at one with the wall, Bert began talking about his life. He was so interesting and funny, hearing all about his very eventful life was a great distraction from having to swear at the useless steamer! Amidst one of his stories, Anne decided to join them for a dance.

'Dancing time Bert,' she said, taking hold of his hands, expecting him to instantly swirl her around.

'Another one that is completely crackers, Anne this is Will. He is going to be spending some time with us here, working on smartening the place up.'

'Hello Will, do you like to dance?' she asked, still trying to get Bert to start moving.

'Actually I have learnt to like it a bit, wasn't sure at first though,' he replied.

'You are too blimmin young to know our type of dancing though, it's not the disco stuff you know that she likes,' said Bert.

And with that, Will climbed down the step ladder, put the steamer on the floor (he could do with a break anyway as it was starting to drive him mad) and took hold of Anne's hands. 'Come on Anne, my turn,' he said and started moving around the floor with her.

'Oh my goodness you are wonderful, like Cary Grant!' she said beaming and closing her eyes as they danced.

Simon was just making a staff tea run and had just popped his head around the door to see if Will was ready for his next cuppa. He quietly watched as Will whisked her around the floor and as they finished, Will took a bow as Anne curtsied, thanking each other for the dance. Hearing clapping, they all turned to see Simon beaming from ear to ear. 'Well that was just lovely, made my day that has. Cuppa Will?' he asked and left with goosebumps, saying to himself that it is so weird but so right how things turn out sometimes.

Will settled in so well everywhere he went. He got to know the locals at the shops and spent most evenings grabbing something to eat and drink at the pub before crashing out. He and Alf spoke a few evenings a week to check on each other, pleased everything was going well at both ends and Max of course was ok too. He really missed

Max, but he wouldn't be allowed at the B&B and not being around much, it would have been unfair on him. He was much better off where he was. Everyone at Green Meadows was so friendly and welcoming, he really felt like part of the team. Anne had been telling some of the other ladies about him too, so most days he would be interrupted for *'just a quick dance please Will,'* which he didn't really mind and it seemed to cheer them up no end.

A few days later he began getting regular visits from Margaret, one of their newest residents. Whilst her daughter-in-law Sarah had been taking amazing care of her for some time now, reluctantly she had had to put her into care. Sarah had been struggling with a young baby and her mother-in-law's dementia getting worse and worse - she was so upset but knew it was right for her to move into Green Meadows. Margaret had settled in really well and seemed to be enjoying the routine and activities, which reassured Sarah that she had made the right decision. She still came to see her regularly.

Margaret seemed happy and chatty, whilst confusing Will for her son. Calling out 'Brian!' when she entered the room, expecting him to answer, she got a bit annoyed when he didn't.

'Can you not hear me?' she exclaimed.

And Will quickly realised that it didn't really matter that he wasn't Brian and it didn't help saying no and trying to explain. Instead he would quickly answer with 'are you ready for a dance?' as a distraction, which always worked and seemed to make her very happy. She then talked about her husband and how she met him at a dance, *'love at first sight exists you know,'* she would say every time. 'Are you married or have you got a girlfriend?' she once asked.

'Not yet,' he replied.

'Is there something wrong with you?' she replied, pulling a funny face.

'No, just not really made time for relationships yet, been too busy,' he would always answer, not elaborating on the fact that in reality he was also waiting for the right person who he simply hadn't met yet.

The staff would then come and rescue him and take her off to do something else, but loving the fact that Will would always make the time for her.

The wallpaper was finally off and Will was clearing away his tools ready to go home, when he suddenly heard 'Brian, Brian!' being called out from the corridor. As the voice was getting closer and closer he resigned himself to the fact, whilst he felt completely shattered and just wanted to jump in the bath for a soak, one last dance was on the cards before he left. Smiling to himself, Margaret came flying around the corner, nearly losing her balance and he quickly rushed to whisk her up. 'Steady Margaret, you won't be able to dance if you fall and break your leg or something!' he exclaimed, smiling at her.

'I thought you might have gone already, wanted to catch you before you left. I just wanted to tell you about how I met my dear Ron, is that ok?' she asked, with the kindest smile.

'Of course, I'd love to hear all about it. So what happened then, how did you meet?' he asked, even though he had heard the story many times already. One of the things dear Mabel had drummed into him as a child was the importance of truly listening to show you care. She would tell him *'it is one of the loveliest things you can do for someone and a way to show you really genuinely care. Listen, don't interrupt and really listen to what and how they are saying what they are talking about. As if it's the first time you have ever heard it. When people want to tell you something that is really important to them, these conversations often don't need an answer, unless of course they ask for one. If you are so busy thinking of your response or experience and butting in to interrupt, you're not really listening.'* And she was so right. With the room nearly cleared ready for the next day, Will took a seat next to Margaret and looked at her while she reminisced. He had only recently put a few chairs in the room with him, ready to give his unexpected visitors somewhere safe to sit.

As she was nearing the finale about how Ron had then asked her for another date and told her '*you know we are going to get married someday and be the happiest couple, you'll see*' which made her giggle and tear up a bit too, there was suddenly an odd rumbling noise coming around the door. And in flew the cutest little girl in her walker, quickly followed by her mum.

'Lily, blimey you are getting the hang of this a bit too much!' she called out, then looking around suddenly realised she wasn't on her own.

'Oh so sorry to interrupt,' and then looking up properly, 'Margaret! How lovely to see you, you're looking so well,' she said, grabbing Lily in her walker and wheeling her over to them. 'Lily, come and see Grandma.'

'Alison, how lovely to see you,' Margaret replied, getting up from her chair to go and give her a hug. 'Come and meet Brian.'

Sarah walked over to Will to shake hands, 'Nice to meet you Brian,' she said, as Will mouthed '*it's Will actually.*' She started laughing, and whispered '*and I'm Sarah by the way, not Allison, but doesn't matter does it,*' and they both smiled at each other. 'And this is Lily,' she said as Will bent down to say hello to Lily.

'Nice to meet you too Lily,' and she managed to break free of Sarah's grip and zoom off around the room, her walker wheels speeding up. Luckily apart from the few chairs, and with Will's tools up on the one of the windowsills, she had a massive space to enjoy her new found independence! Getting the hang of turning around, she was squealing with laughter. Sarah took a seat next to Margaret and Will, while they caught each other up on their past few days' activities.

'How are things in London?' asked Margaret.

'Yes, all good thanks. Pretty much the same as always,' Sarah replied.

'And Mr & Mrs Harris - still running the corner shop?' she asked.

'Yes, they are both well and busy with the shop as always,' replied Sarah.

She had long stopped reminding her that they had moved out of London a couple of years ago to the countryside. It had been Brian's idea. Her only child, he had of course insisted that as her health had deteriorated, she must move in with them for them to take care of her. Sarah was only too pleased to agree to this. She had no idea the toll dementia would have and was totally unprepared for what lay ahead.

* * *

Always being a city girl, she wasn't sure how she would cope with life in the countryside but with Brian moving onto piloting short haul flights, he would be around a lot. She was sceptical but trusted everything would be ok. With the money they got for the house in London, they bought a huge house set in three acres of lawns and woodland. A little stream ran through the woods at the bottom of the garden, and with the external of the house being mainly glass, she felt like she had landed in a magazine shoot. 'It is lovely, but aren't we a bit isolated up here? Wouldn't it be better to buy somewhere in the village down the road?' she had asked Brian while they were on their second viewing of the property, and him about to agree an offer with the estate agent.

'Think of the fresh air and privacy though! I thought you would be really chuffed Sarah, for goodness sake. Can't believe you are finding fault with it!' he replied, miffed.

'Oh sorry, yes I'm sure you're right. And it's only a mile down the road, so not far. And with you home more, it will be lovely. Loads of room for your mum and no busy roads to worry about,' she said, feeling a little tearful but inside trying to convince herself that of course he was right.

It had been a quick move and at the same time she found out she was pregnant too. 'See, lots of fresh air for our baby - told you it was a good idea!' said Brian, cuddling her in the kitchen one night shortly after they moved in. Then suddenly hearing some crashing went charging off to see what his mum was up to.

The first six months were idyllic and with Brian home more often to help with his mum, life was turning out well. Pregnancy progressed well and she had loved every minute, especially when the kicking had started. The birth on the other hand had been completely traumatic. Whilst their little girl had eventually arrived into the world completely healthy, Sarah had been through the mill. So whilst Lily was having her first cuddles with dad, Sarah was left sucking on gas and air for the stitching that was required.

A few days later at home Sarah had just got off the phone. 'Bloody hell, they need to start sending you home with a supply of gas and air for when you want to try sitting down or going for a wee! The midwife has just asked if I have done a number two yet - I told her you have got to be joking! There is absolutely no way that is happening anytime soon!' she said, trying to laugh, even though it wasn't really funny. Brian passed her a glass of wine which disappeared instantly, ready for a top up.

At the local shops she spotted a beach rubber ring covered in dust, 'perfect' she thought buying it, much to the shopkeepers delight. 'God knows why they had it in stock as there's no beach nearby but lucky for me,' she said to herself whilst wiping off the dust and taking a tentative sit down with it on the sofa. *'Not perfect but definitely helps, especially while I need to calmly feed Lily.'* Occasionally it would disappear, and she would find Margaret with it in her bath, which always made her laugh. She was such a lovely mother-in-law, not her fault that she was losing her marbles. She loved being with her and Lily; her own little family even though it was hard work with being left in sole charge of both of them more and more often.

Whilst Brian had always promised that he would stay on short haul to be able to spend more time at home, this had started changing. While everything was taking a while to repair, Brian was getting increasingly frustrated at the lack of intimacy and how she was always tired. Sarah tried her best but explained how even wearing pants was still so painful so he would have to be patient, and maybe if he could help a bit with the night shifts she wouldn't feel so completely shattered all the time. A bit of help with cooking and housework wouldn't go amiss either, which usually resulted with the dog being yanked out of his bed for a walk and the slamming of the backdoor as they left.

Sarah had met him as long haul cabin crew and that is how their relationship started. With these flights requiring you to be away from home more often than not, the down time spent in the destination country had always been a lot of fun. With expenses paid, it was generally party time for everyone until the return journey a few days later. Normally you very rarely got to be on the same flight as crew you had worked with previously, but once they had begun their relationship Brian seemed to be able to pull strings to ensure she was in the crew on most of his flights. They saw lots of the world together and everything had been great. When his dad passed away, he kept closer tabs on his mum and once she was showing signs of not coping very well, felt the best place for her was to move in with them. Their wedding followed, which was a beautiful day. However shortly after, a doctor's appointment with his mum confirmed their fears that her memory was deteriorating and not just a symptom of grief. Lily then arrived in a rather dramatic way - massive ouch!

A couple of months after she was born, Brian arrived home with a massive bouquet of flowers, which Margaret thanked him for and hurried off to get a vase for her bedroom. Of course, they were actually for Sarah to cushion the news he was about to deliver. With Lily in her cot, he poured them both a large glass of wine and set about telling Sarah that he had made the difficult decision to go back to long haul flights.

'But what about us? And your Mum? And you moved me out to the countryside to spend more time together you said!' as she threw the half-filled glass in his face. 'You selfish git! All I asked was for a bit of help. But no, just thinking of yourself, you leave me to do everything as always!' she screamed at him, at which point Margaret appeared.

'Is there a problem? Have I done something wrong?' she asked, concerned.

'Oh no Margaret, everything is fine. Sorry didn't mean for you to hear that. Shall I get you a drink as Coronation Street is about to start?' Sarah replied quickly. Looking at Brian, she said firmly, 'Wait here, this conversation isn't finished yet!' and left to sort out Margaret.

Arriving back in the kitchen to see the dog and lead gone, she sat at the island, poured another glass of wine and burst into tears. 'I just can't do everything on my own anymore,' she sobbed. Glugging the wine quickly and with a lack of food and sleep, started feeling tipsy very fast. Looking down into her glass, tears pouring down her cheeks trying to fill it back up again, she suddenly felt a warm embrace across her shoulders.

'It will be alright you know,' said Margaret, giving her the warmest hug she had had in ages. 'I know I get mixed up sometimes, but don't think in my confusion that I am not very aware of what is happening and see all that you do. If I had had a daughter I would have wished her to be exactly like you,' she said, with tears now pouring down her face.

Turning around to hug her back, she said 'Thank you Margaret. You are like a mum to me - I feel truly blessed to have you in my life you know,' filling up two glasses with wine.

'I am sorry I have this stupid dementia, I truly am, as could be so much more support to you otherwise. I never want to be a burden you know and if and when I go downhill, please know that I would like you to find a home for me to move to. Come and see me if you can, but never feel guilty about it, will you promise me that?' she said, eyes pleading with her.

In moments like this, Sarah just wanted to curl up in the dark somewhere. Yes, Margaret was getting progressively worse but she still had lots of moments like now and she couldn't bear the thought of putting her somewhere else to live. The only nice thing was that she didn't seem to realise how much worse she had got, which Sarah thought was a blessing and tried her best to make the most of times like now. Also, Margaret and Lily seemed to have a particularly special connection. If she was particularly distressed about something that she and no-one else could fathom, Lily's arrival always seemed to calm everything. Lily could also be screaming the house down but when put in the arms of Margaret, would immediately settle.

Margaret went back to her room just as Brian reappeared. Looking at her like she was the one with the problem, he said 'I mean it's not as though we see much of each other now is it? You are always flying around sorting out mum, Lily and the house; you will probably hardly notice that I'm not here anyway! The extra money will be handy too, won't it?!'

'You just don't bloody get it do you! Do you ever think of asking if you could do anything? When I ask you to help me, you just seem to get distracted and forget or are too busy. We don't need the money, all we want is some of your time, is that too much to ask?!' she replied, sobbing.

Brian's answer to confrontation was always the same; grab car keys or dog lead and leave the house. With the dog looking exhausted from the unexpected evening walk he had just had, Brian grabbed the keys and was gone.

In the early hours of the following morning, Sarah found him downstairs on the sofa asleep as she warmed Lily's bottle. Looking at him while it warmed, rocking Lily in her arms, she wondered how she could change things or improve them. Had she known their relationship was going to take such a massive nosedive, for a start she would never have agreed to move to the middle of bloody nowhere! Things were frosty for the next few days, until she apologised. Later that evening after sorting everyone and everything thing out, she slumped down on the sofa and watched as Brian came across to sit with her, pouring her a glass of their favourite chardonnay. The rest of the evening, with Margaret and Lily both fast asleep for a change, they had a lovely time together, laughing and cuddling while getting merry, before falling into bed together. See things could be better she thought, *'maybe if I just keep schtum and get on with it, it will all be ok, maybe I have just become a bit of a boring nag!'*

The next day Brian got up early and for the first time let Sarah sleep in, while he took Lily downstairs for her milk. Margaret joined him soon after and Sarah woke later - after having had more than three hours sleep in one hit she felt like she could take on the world! It was a glorious sunny day, so they all spent the morning in the garden. Brian then offered to get a picnic lunch ready for them to have down by the stream at the bottom of the garden. Sarah, Margaret and Lily setup the large blanket and lay in the shade of the huge willow tree. Brian seemed to take ages but Sarah stopped herself from going up there to see how he was doing, *'must try and chill a bit and appreciate what he is doing'* she told herself. About an hour and a half later, Brian arrived with lunch. They all tucked in and enjoyed their first family picnic together as Brian so rarely could join them. And as they all finished and began packing the bits up, to take back to the house and put Lily down for her afternoon nap, Brian announced that he would be leaving tonight for his long haul flight to Australia. He would be back in sixteen days time but said he would of course phone when he got there.

Margaret had a lot to say about this, ending with 'Your dad would be so disappointed with your decision – we raised you to put your family first.' There was of course no changing his mind.

Brian stomped off and returned very quickly with two suitcases.

'Oh my god! That's why it took you so long to get the picnic ready – you were packing your bloody suitcases!' exclaimed Sarah.

'There's no point in discussing it anymore – I'm going and that's that! I'm not putting up with your bloody selfishness!' he shouted and went back inside. Two minutes later they heard the front door slam. He didn't even stop to give them a hug or kiss goodbye, not even Lily.

In the months that followed, Sarah found life harder and harder. While Lily became a little easier and at last started giving something back, making her and Margaret nearly wet themselves laughing when she got the unstoppable giggles at so many things, Brian spent more and more time at work. Often phoning to say he needed to cover a pilot's flight as they'd called in sick, he came home less and less.

Margaret's mental state was also getting worse. It wasn't just the forgetfulness, or not being sure what she was supposed to be doing, but the much more alarming wandering off. Sarah always did her best to check she had locked the front and back doors, after Margaret was found wandering in the village down the road with no idea where she was, and brought back by the local policeman. Luckily he had got out of her that the house had lots of massive windows, and looking like a property from one of the modern home design shows on TV, guessed it had to be theirs. So now, even though it was the height of summer and boiling hot, all windows and doors had to be kept locked shut. Lily was teething which meant more sleepless nights and stinking nappies piling high in the bin.

One morning Sarah came down with her to find Margaret had taken all the nappies out of the bin and placed them like stepping stones around the kitchen. She had already cut her own hair on one side, had three breakfasts and was now giggling at the game she had made up. 'Come on!' she called out, 'see if you can jump onto the stones without touching the floor!' As she jumped onto one of the worst ones, the diarrhoea squirted up her trousers and across the floor. 'Goodness, these stones stink don't they! Might need a clothes peg,' she giggled, pinching her nose.

Sarah could either laugh or cry. And for a change, decided on laughter. Once she started, she just couldn't stop as the floor and Margaret were increasingly covered in poo! Probably looking like she should be admitted to a funny farm, she just sat there laughing her head off with Margaret, who was also finding it hysterically funny. Lily had for a minute gone incredibly quiet before she joined in too. If only they had had a video camera!

After a few minutes and realising the cleanup operation was getting more and more extensive, Sarah went into the lounge and put Margaret's favourite film in the video recorder. Grabbing Margaret a drink and getting her cleaned up and a new pair of trousers and tights, she helped her get changed and then showed her to the sofa. She then set about cleaning all the mess and opening the windows while it was safe to do so. Margaret's hair looked horrendous and who knows what was going on with her makeup. Then she suddenly shuddered, thinking of what else could have happened with the scissors and other things in the kitchen. Sitting on the floor amongst poo and nappies, the laughter soon changed to tears as she realised that the inevitable was going to have to happen sooner rather than later. She worried that she couldn't guarantee to keep her safe. She rang Brian's phone and left a message, as she needed his agreement to start looking. Two days it took him to reply, saying of course mum would understand that it was best for her and he would be happy with whatever her choice of home was, there was no point in any delay and waiting for him to come and help choose.

Confiding in her health visitor at the doctor's surgery in the village, she instantly said Green Meadows was where everyone around here wanted to go if you could get a place. 'The best care you could wish for and we have all asked for a provisional booking ourselves for when the time comes,' were her words and so Sarah made the call.

After meeting Simon and the rest of the team and looking around, she knew Margaret would be really well looked after and would have someone around the clock to see that she was ok. And fortunately, whilst it really upset her to do it, Margaret seemed to be thriving. Home though was increasingly lonely. Brian's flight schedule seemed to have increased massively, which he apparently couldn't turn down. The financial benefits couldn't always be felt either as apparently while the number of flights had increased, he had to take the hit on some of them as the flying hours were needed to keep his commercial licence.

So life for Sarah and Lily revolved around keeping themselves as busy as possible with trips to the local village and visits to Margaret, and trying to enjoy the occasional dad/husband time at home. The countryside and fresh air was beautiful, that was in no doubt, and the local people were really friendly, thank god. But it definitely wasn't the life she had envisaged, feeling like a single parent.

Dashing in through the door to the phone ringing, she got to it just too late and the answer machine clicked in. Grabbing her bags and putting Lily on the floor, she listened to hear the message enquiring as to whether Brian was well enough yet to confirm his next flight schedule, commencing in two days time. Please could he confirm by the end of the day or they would have to get cover from another pilot. Sitting on the floor next to Lily completely dumbstruck, she tried not to get carried away with the bad thoughts that had already entered her brain. '*Must be a good reason, maybe he is going to surprise us with a visit?*' she tried to persuade herself, unconvincingly. She quickly grabbed the phone and called him - as always there was no answer so she left a message. An hour or so later he phoned her back, saying that there must have been a mix up as he had already confirmed his flight schedule and was in London awaiting his next flight out in about two hours time. '*Useless personnel staff, always messing up,*' he reassured her and said he would phone her again when he landed in Thailand. But the nagging thoughts she already had, had only increased now.

After another month of little time at home, she couldn't help herself but hated the person he had changed her into; checking his pockets and clothes. He had already got in the habit of changing and emptying his case the minute he got home, putting everything in the wash under the pretence of realising he needed to help out a bit more, at least when he was at home anyway. But he was also so distant, with longer dog walks and popping out into the garden when his phone rang. One evening after a few too many glasses of wine, she finally plucked up the courage to ask him outright, 'Are you having an affair?'

'Oh my god, how could you say that! You know I've been thinking for a while that you could do with getting a doctor's appointment and see about getting some tablets for depression. Apparently lots of new mums find it overwhelming and get low, and you must agree you have found it very hard haven't you!' he answered firmly.

'I do not need bloody tablets thank you! A husband and dad for our baby wouldn't go amiss though! How dare you! You always try and put it back on me, well no more!' she shouted in reply.

'Christ, keep your bloody hair on! You know, I would never have thought you would change so much Sarah, it's such a shame. Your drinking seems to have increased too.'

'I think you will find I haven't changed at all, well apart from caring a bit more about what matters. You on the other hand, I feel like I don't know you anymore or maybe I never really did know the real you. And it's nothing to do with the drink, it just gives me the courage to say what I really think,' she said with tears trickling down her cheeks. And on cue, with no hug or reassurance, the dog lead was taken off the hook and the dog dragged out for another late night walk.

Brian had taken to sleeping in Margaret's old room, to avoid disturbing Sarah when he came in, sometimes late into the night. It also used to coincide with Lily being poorly and Sarah moving her cot into their room – saying he didn't want to disturb either of them and needed to get some good sleep due to jetlag.

So with another packed schedule and just finding out as he left, that he wouldn't be back for six weeks this time, Sarah closed the door and walked over to the window. Looking out into the most picturesque garden, she sighed and prayed that life would get better - it had to. Maybe it was Brian that was struggling to cope as a new parent, as it was proving hard. Maybe he was also worrying deep down about his mum and grieving for the mum he was losing to dementia. Opening the door and walking out onto the grass, she said 'Come on Lily, let's go and feed the birds and then see Grandma. Show her your new wheels!' Putting her down onto the grass to crawl off at great speed, they headed for the bird table.

* * *

'Look at her! Isn't she fast, expect she will be walking soon!' exclaimed Margaret, as Lily whizzed up to them.

'Gosh hope it's not too soon though - at least I know where she is at the moment,' Sarah replied smiling.

'How old is she?' Will asked.

'Ten months. It sometimes feels like longer than that, blame that on lack of sleep though. She is lovely but gosh, it's hard work,' she replied. 'How are you getting on here Margaret?'

All she needed at this point was constant reassurance that the decision she had made was the right one.

'Oh really good thank you. And I get to dance too you know,' Margaret replied, dreamily.

'Really? I didn't realise you liked dancing so much, who is your dance partner?' asked Sarah.

'You're sat next to him! Want to see us?' she asked excitedly.

'Well of course, I would love that!' replied Sarah, smiling at Will quizzically.

Blushing slightly, Will got up and took hold of Margaret's hand, 'I'm not that good, and feel a bit embarrassed with an audience but oh well, here goes.' As he slowly waltzed with Margaret around the floor, Lily thought this was really funny and chased after them in her wheels. When they had finished, Will bowed and took Margaret by the hand back to sit with Sarah. Sarah beamed with delight, as she could see how happy she was and for the first time in a while she could picture Margaret as the young and carefree lady she once was.

'That's a really lovely thing to do, thank you,' Sarah said to Will smiling and with Lily disappearing around the corner, left to chase after her. Margaret went to find them while Will collected his bag and jacket and headed for the door to go home.

Simon wanted a quick chat with him before he left about some unexpected problems with the plumbing and to see if he could help, so by the time he got to the door, Sarah and Lily were also saying their goodbyes.

'See you again soon Margaret,' she said, giving her a big hug and kiss. Lily then gave her a big wet kiss and waving goodbye, they walked out to the car.

Clicking her into her car seat, she spotted Will just walking off down the drive. Calling out, she offered him a lift, which he happily accepted as he was completely shattered from such a busy day. She dropped him off at his bed and breakfast, thanking him again for the care he had shown Margaret and telling him how it had helped reassure her even more that she had made the right decision.

The jobs at the care home were increasing daily. While old buildings are lovely, their maintenance is also never ending, especially when nothing has been done for quite some time. So Alf had agreed that, as everything was working out well, he and Max were happy at Primrose so there was no rush for Will to come back yet - he should stay on and try and get everything running smoothly. Will would try to pop back on Sundays to see them both and have a bit of down time. There was always something lovely about being back home with your own stuff. The B&B was great, but you were just a guest.

The local pub in the village however loved having their new regular customer, who didn't just prop up the bar as he always required a meal too! The locals at the bar were all really friendly and, like all villagers, knew everything that was going on. The gossip and ribbing in the evenings proved to be a great source of entertainment. There were just three local lads at the pool table that weren't so popular. Hogging it every night so no-one else could have a game, if you put your money on the side of the table they would knock it on the floor.

'If Robbie's dad wasn't in charge of the local police station, I would give him a good thrashing. That's what he bloody needs, jumped up little shit that one,' Roger muttered to Will as he waited to get another pint at the bar. 'Robbie's the one in the middle! The other two, Steve and Gary, are harmless - wouldn't do anything if he wasn't around.'

'There's always someone that ruins it, isn't there,' replied Will, and clocked them to remember their faces.

A few days later he was in the hardware store collecting some supplies, when the subject of those three came up again. 'Just to give you a heads up Will, but there are three lads that I wouldn't trust with a bargepole. One of them moved back here recently, fell out with his mum apparently so back with dad. Just keep an eye on your stuff, as your tools are worth a pretty packet. I mean, normally here you can leave your back door open all day even when you pop out, but there are some odd things happening that have just started since his arrival. The local newsagent's stock is suddenly down and we suspect it has something to do with him. Might be a coincidence but not worth taking the risk, just so you know,' the store owner said, looking concerned.

'Thanks for that. To be honest I have occasionally left my car unlocked as it seemed like the safest place in the world here. Won't now though,' he replied smiling and left the store.

He popped into the chippy a few nights later, as decided to have a night off the beer, when he was joined in the queue by the delightful three. Pushing and shoving each other, acting like complete dickheads, they then helped themselves to a can of drink each, swigging it down and putting the empty cans on the small table. Will could feel his heart rate beginning to rise straight away. Trying to keep his gob shut, one of them suddenly bumped into the back of him. 'Eh steady, watch it!' he said to him sternly.

'Alright, only a bloody accident!' Robbie replied.

'And what can I get you Will?' the chip shop owner suddenly intervened.

'Standard fish and chips please Derek,' he replied, trying his hardest to ignore them - it wasn't worth it.

Handing over his money and taking his meal and change, he turned and left to hear them refuse to pay for the cans. 'Wasn't us?' they said laughing, 'prove it!'

'I saw you drink them,' Will said, making his way back to the counter.

'I'd keep that nose and gob out of it if I were you,' snarled Robbie again and with the owner shaking his head, inferring to leave it, Will walked out fuming.

Talking to himself walking back to the car, it took him the fish and chips and a whole episode of Eastenders before he calmed down. Lying on his bed, it took him longer than usual to get to sleep especially with no alcohol to assist.

The next night he updated the regulars at the pub with his encounter at the chippy.

'Bloody hell Derek can't afford for people not to pay. It's hard enough to make ends meet as it is. Maybe we should report them to the police, even if his dad is chief, doesn't mean nothing should happen,' said Roger. They all agreed they would look out for each other and the other villagers too - no way was some jumped up little twerp going to waltz in and ruin their village. And after sharing with everyone what had happened, Will thought maybe he could change his routine slightly, benefitting Derek and his liver, by one evening a week having fish and chips rather than his usual pub meal.

At the care home the next day on the other hand, he had a very welcome new visitor. Standing at the top of the step ladder painting the wall, he suddenly heard the door creak open and turned to see little Lily crawling as fast as she could with a biscuit in her hand. Quickly climbing back down, he popped his paint and roller on the side and was ready at the bottom step as she reached him.

Smiling at him and handing him her biscuit, she was insistent that maybe it should go in his mouth. Making lots of little noises and with her arms up in the air to be picked up, he bent down and whisked her up in his arms. Just as she was now ramming the biscuit into his lips, which was making him laugh, Sarah appeared.

'Oh I'm so sorry. One minute I was looking at some photos with Margaret thinking she was happily playing on the floor, and the next minute she's gone!'

'Honestly don't worry – it's nice to have a break anyway, even though I might not fancy eating her mushed biscuit!' he replied smiling. And with that, she shoved it hard into his mouth giving him no choice.

Sarah laughed and Lily did too, as she tried to get him to have another bite.

Taking her off him, Lily was having none of it and screamed until she passed her back.

'Think someone has a fan, don't you?!' said Sarah smiling.

'She's incredibly cute isn't she,' he replied, as Lily then put her head firmly on his chest and clung to him.

'Come on Lily, Will has got lots to do!' said Sarah, trying to prise her off him. Luckily Margaret appeared calling *'Lily my darling'* and she wriggled to get down and was off to see her grandma.

'See you again soon, I'm sure,' said Sarah smiling as she walked off to the door.

'You are welcome anytime,' replied Will.

The following week, on his night off from the pub, Will was sitting in the park with his fish and chips when he heard some voices. Hearing some wheels on the gravel, Lily and Sarah suddenly appeared around the corner.

'Oh hi Will,' Sarah called out as she wheeled Lily towards the swings.

'Hi you two,' he called back.

The minute her seatbelt was un-clicked and she was free, she crawled at great speed across the grass to Will. Arriving at his feet, with Sarah tutting behind her, she said 'Can't get away from us can you?!'

'Is she allowed chips?' he asked, as Lily pulled herself up clinging onto his trousers.

'Don't think she has tried one yet, come to think of it,' but with that Lily was at Will's hand like a little bird with her mouth wide open.

Blowing on it to make sure it wasn't too hot, he popped the end of it in her mouth. Chomp and it was gone, with a mouth wide open for some more please.

'Lily – it's Will's tea!' exclaimed Sarah. 'Sorry about this, you would think I didn't feed her!'

'Nice to have some company – take a seat,' he replied smiling and picked Lily up to sit on his lap.

She happily sat there for nearly twenty minutes, eating bits of chip and fish, while Sarah and Will chatted about their days and dear Margaret. When it was all gone, while Sarah carried her over to the swings, he scrunched the newspaper up and popped it in the litter bin before joining them.

It was such a lovely, fun, relaxing hour they spent together – totally unexpected but very welcome. Saying their goodbyes to head home, he got a massive cuddle from Lily who was also insistent that he put her in her car seat. Giving him a little wave goodbye, he wandered back to the B&B feeling very content with the world.

But a few nights later, cutting through the park on his way to the pub, Will was greeted by a nasty smell. Turning the corner, he found Robbie and his mates sitting on the bench smoking weed. Keeping his head down and trying not to make eye contact, he hurried through before one of them started shouting obscenities. 'Fucking weirdo you are mate, spending all your time with the old gits of this place. What's the matter with you? Maybe you're just pretending to be nice and then trying to get them to change their wills to leave everything to you; maybe I need to sow some seeds with my dad to keep any eye on you. Wouldn't be hard to stitch you up either!' he shouted at him while the others just sniggered.

'Believe it or not, some people actually care about others rather than just looking out for themselves. Grow up you idiot!' Will shouted back and then hearing movement, hastily sped up down the path.

'Yeah, run off to the old codgers at the bar! Better watch your back!' Robbie shouted back at Will.

The first pint was downed in an instant.

'Blimey someone's thirsty!' said Roger smiling.

'Those three idiots were in the park and just had a slight run in with them. Sat there, thinking they own the place, smoking their drugs. Surely the local police just can't sit by and let them get away with doing whatever they want. They must at least have to record it and even caution them about unacceptable behaviour or something?!' he asked, looking around at the three locals sat at the bar.

'Good luck trying. Probably better just to keep schtum and hope he gets bored and moves on. Or his mum decides he needs to move back in with her. That's what we are all hoping for,' was the reply.

They had become quite the talk of the village, with lots of muttering everywhere you went. Even at the care home, they took extra measures to make sure every window, door and all the outside buildings were kept locked at all times. No-one wanted any unwelcome visitors.

On Sarah's visits to see Margaret she had also heard some rumours, and with Brian very rarely home was feeling particularly vulnerable being so secluded. She quickly found a local CCTV specialist in the next town and paid a premium for cameras and lighting to be fitted. *'If Brian can't be here then he can bloody pay out for this for us, sorry couldn't check with you first but you never answer your phone,'* she said to herself smiling as she ordered the most expensive system, putting it on his credit card.

Once it was all kitted out, with one camera scanning the front of the house and two cameras scanning the back, she sat with a glass of wine in the evening starting to feel much more relaxed. She always double checked the doors and windows were locked anyway before she went to bed, having grown up in the city.

Will had been really helpful too, and offered to help with anything needed. That was the good thing about village life; people really did look out for each other.

A few evenings later, Will and the others were sat at the bar having their daily catch up and piss take, when in sauntered Robbie and Gary. Getting their pints, they wandered over to the pool table like they owned the place. Calling over to the barman, Robbie said 'Bloody hell, are there no decent girls in this place. Is there any chance of meeting anyone under the age of seventy?'

A couple of older ladies sitting at a table quickly looked down, sipping their gin and tonics, looked terribly uncomfortable.

'Ay, ay, that's enough now! No-one says you have to come and drink in here, or even live here come to think of it. You haven't exactly made yourself welcome have you!' snapped the barman.

'Oh look who it is! Perfect for that idiot at the bar, seems he only likes spending time with old codgers. Watch out ladies, he probably wants to get in your knickers, the perv!' shouted Robbie in reply.

Will had to be held back from attacking him. 'Just ignore them Will, this is what they want and then daddy gets called and you get a criminal record! It's not worth it over a little scrote like that!' Roger said, holding him by the shoulders. The ladies just smiled at Will, shaking their heads in dismay.

After a few minutes of silence and drinks being downed quicker than expected, glasses were refilled and the chatter started again, ignoring the lads now playing pool.

Life at the care home and B&B was flying past and Will had quickly become part of the village, it surprised him how much he enjoyed this part too. He had generally always kept his head down and tried not to stand out or be noticed. But here there was no chance of not being noticed and people really wanted to chat, which was refreshingly different and actually quite nice.

All the carers, residents and visitors to the care home were always chatty and fun, and he had gained quite a reputation on the dance floor. He still didn't feel particularly comfortable doing it, but they really seemed to get a lot out of it, and as long as he didn't have too much of an audience, his cheeks didn't change colour too much!

Sarah and Lily were the home's most regular visitors, and being twenty-four years old, a year younger than Will, they found they had lots in common. Whilst Margaret often got them muddled for someone else, she absolutely adored them coming and the time they were together made all the difference to her wellbeing. She always perked up after their visits.

Will had finally completed the redecoration of the large room which had been disused for many years. Simon was toying with a few ideas of how to actually use the space. A few of the residents' mental state had been deteriorating recently, causing much mayhem and them to get quite agitated. 'How about we style it with old fashioned type items, as isn't that what seems to help calm them and they are at their happiest, when they are reminiscing?' Will suggested.

'That's actually a great idea. I love the way Angie has their room at Primrose - especially for all the activities and children's visits but our residents have more complex needs don't they? If we could make at least part of it into a calming space, we would all benefit. Any ideas of what we should put in it, anyone?' Simon asked, looking around at the team members in the room.

'Is it time for the bus yet?!' asked Betty urgently, suddenly appearing around the door.

'Five minutes yet, come on, let's find your chair!' Michelle one of the carers said smiling, taking her by the arm to find the chair. This always relaxed Betty before she could carry on with the day again.

Suddenly remembering the cupboard full of old things back at home, and the last of the furniture that he hadn't manage to sell, Will had an idea and offered to help, if someone could get hold of a van. He also spoke with Alf later that evening, to see if he was up to doing some woodwork, which of course he was and couldn't wait to help.

The following weekend, Simon and Will got up early and chugged down the roads in the van Simon had managed to get hold of. 'Blimey, hope you're not paying too much for this!' exclaimed Will, as he frantically opened the window to try and get some fresh air. Fusty was the understatement of the century, and he burst out laughing as Simon nearly jumped out of his skin as it suddenly backfired, expelling a massive cloud of smoke.

'Christ, I hope this old thing makes it there and back! One of the farmers leant it to me, been in his yard not doing much, so no charge apart from the diesel,' Simon laughed, with his window down fully too. With a top speed of 35mph it was going to take longer than expected, and they hadn't allowed for the old back tyre to decide to deflate and leave them stranded in the middle of nowhere. By the time they walked and found a farm, phoned the local garage and got a new tyre fitted most of the day was gone. They finally reached Will's house, to be greeted by a very excited Max, by early evening.

Introducing him to Alf and Max, they decided that after the day they had had, they would have some grub and a few beers, load up the van but stay overnight and travel back in the morning. Simon rang the home to let them know what was happening, and Will popped down the road to grab them fish, chips and a couple of beers each.

They had a really fun evening together and Simon couldn't believe the furniture and items Will was happy to give to them - he was really touched. 'Are you sure I can't pay you something? This is going to truly transform the room, the residents are going to love it!' he said.

'Honestly I'm just pleased it's going to have a new home somewhere it will be appreciated, rather than shut away here gathering dust,' Will replied.

Will had asked Alf not to mention the woodwork project to Simon, as it would be a great surprise for everyone. Later that evening Alf secretly showed Will what he had made. As always, Will was completely blown away when he saw the wooden bus stop and bench, ready for installation! 'Blimey Alf, that is amazing!' he exclaimed, putting his arm around Alf's shoulders as they both admired his handiwork.

'I am pretty chuffed with this one actually, really enjoyed doing it too. Maybe me and Max could pop up and visit when you are finished,' replied Alf, beaming.

'We would love that!' replied Will.

Whilst everyone was catching up with each other's lives in Will's house, Sarah had just said goodbye to Margaret and decided to walk home via the park. As it wasn't late, she decided to let Lily have a go on the swings before going home for tea. Unfortunately for her, she had company.

Wolf whistling as she passed them sat on the bench, Sarah just completely ignored them and headed for the swings.

'Oi!' shouted Robbie. Sniggering to the other two, he said 'About bloody time. Thought there were only old codgers and mingers in this place. This one, on the other hand, looks just like my type. Shame she's got herself knocked up already though, kids can get in the way,' he said, through his tobacco stained teeth.

Showing off to his mates, he sauntered over to have a closer look.

'She yours is she? You look too young to have a baby!' he said, trying to act a bit normal. 'Haven't seen you around here before, just moved in recently have you?'

Sarah didn't really want to answer but he looked like he wasn't going anywhere without a response.

'We moved here over a year ago now. My mother-in-law is at Green Meadows,' she said, hoping that realising she was married then, he would bugger off. And it worked.

'Oh right, your old man at home is he? Shame that, was going to invite you out for a drink,' Robbie replied, swaying slightly from the beer he had just finished.

'Yes he is. We had better be getting back now before she starts yelling for her tea,' she said smiling, and quickly putting Lily back in her pushchair, left the park.

Wandering back over to his mates, they were laughing at how his charms were obviously crap!

'Shut your gobs, she's only bloody married!' he said to them to shut them up.

'Yeah we know. Her husband's a pilot, hardly ever there so mum says. She feels sorry for her really, stuck up in that massive house on the hill, all on her own. Apparently she is really nice, mum chats to her in the shop,' Gary informed him. Which got Robbie thinking, maybe he could keep her company later - she might like that!

Hurrying home, Sarah got in the door and started sorting Lily's tea. They had a lovely bath time together, with suds flying all over the bathroom, making Lily squeal with laughter and then mobile on, lights dimmed, time for bed. Baby monitor on and Lily fast asleep in record time, Sarah sat at the island in the kitchen and poured herself a glass of wine. The incident in the park had given her the creeps in a way she hadn't felt since being followed home late one night, when she was sixteen. The only relief was that the place was covered with security now, so she had a little chat to herself about the uneasy feeling she had, told herself to stop being stupid and letting her imagination run away with her. She walked over to the screens, could see clearly that tonight was the same as any other night with nothing around and opened the fridge to pour herself another glass of wine.

Sitting on the sofa with the baby monitor quiet, just the light blinking next to her, she distracted herself with a particularly funny episode of Mrs Merton and was quickly feeling much more relaxed, with the help of a couple of glasses of wine. Down the road, the three lads had spent the evening at the pub and were now pretty drunk. Leaving each other at the phone box to go home, Robbie decided to himself that he had a better idea. He wanted it to be a surprise, so decided to take the quicker route, clambering through the woods.

Yawning her head off, and finding that she must have dozed off as had missed a bit, Sarah turned off the TV, quickly bunged everything in the dishwasher and wandered outside to let the dog have his last wee for the night before final lockup. Taking the baby monitor with her, she wandered after the dog out into the garden. It was a cool evening but not freezing. Suddenly she heard a crackling of twigs and spun around to see tobacco teeth grinning at her.

'Bloody hell, what are you doing here?' she let out in a very alarmed voice.

'Heard you were on your own, thought you might like some company,' he grinned, stinking of weed and beer.

Gulping back nervously, she had to quickly think on her feet. This wasn't a good feeling she was having. 'No, all good here thanks. My husband is just tidying up while I sort out the dog; I think you had best be going home.'

'Nah! Don't think so,' he replied, leering at her. And before she had time to react or run, he shoved her onto the grass. She started to scream but no-one could hear. And as he ripped down her trousers and knickers, she started to struggle and slap him as hard as she could. 'Please don't!' she whimpered. But he took no notice, grabbing a glove out of his coat pocket and ramming it in her mouth, he pinned her to the ground. And with Lily starting to cry on the baby monitor, tears streamed down her cheeks as he raped her. Getting up a few minutes later, with Lily still crying, he just looked at her and said 'Better go and sort your kid hadn't you. Don't want social services thinking you're a bad mother do you? So wouldn't suggest you say anything to anyone about this, I could make your life hell,' he said, threatening her. With that she slapped him hard across the face. 'Wouldn't do that again either, if you know what's good for you!' he said, punching her back so hard in the face she felt momentarily dazed.

He pulled his trousers up and left, staggering back towards the woods. Her dog bounded up to her, licking her face. She couldn't blame him, but really hoped he might have tried to protect her and at least bite him.

Wiping her tears and with Lily now screaming, she pulled up her knickers and trousers, grabbed the dog and the monitor and ran up to the house. Bolting through the door, she ran upstairs and picked up Lily. With both of them sobbing their hearts out, she rocked Lily until she quietened again. Then she ran down to the security screen and quickly rewound the tape. Everything was there.

Quickly grabbing Lily a blanket and bottle, she shoved the tape in her handbag and got in the car. Driving quickly through the lanes, quietly sobbing, she reached the police station within minutes. They weren't used to having anyone arrive late in the evening, so everyone was suddenly alert to this distraught lady and her baby crashing through the door in distress. Being a village police station, they were not really geared up to dealing with a case like this either, but knew they would need to take some samples. Phoning into the police station in the main town, someone arrived within fifteen minutes to assist. Whilst Lily was left in reception, fast asleep in her car seat and ready to be entertained if she woke up, Sarah had the additional trauma of internal examinations. Having only recently completely healed from having Lily, this proved incredibly painful. The police lady kept apologising but she knew this bit was so important and would prove indisputable evidence. They then took her knickers too as evidence, handing her a disposable pair for after the examination was over. After the interview was over, photos taken and the tape submitted, she was comforted by one of the staff and handed a cup of tea. They offered to drive her home but she insisted she was ok, and could drive her and Lily home. They would be in touch tomorrow, the person would be arrested quickly with the amount of evidence they had, they felt sure of that.

And as Sarah and Lily drove back home, the tape was put in the machine. Looking at each other, they were shocked to see the assault and who was involved.

The next morning, the chief police officer arrived as usual with coffee passed to him as he wandered through to his office, when he was updated on the previous evening's events. Watching the tape, his pallor instantly changed. He then asked to be left with the interview notes and all details about this case. *'For fuck's sake Robbie, you might be my son but I'm not sure how I can get you out of this, you bloody idiot!'* he cursed, under his breath to himself. *'The main police station had had some involvement too, shit!'* Then like they had been eavesdropping, the phone rang and he had to take the call.

'No I'm as shocked as everyone that something like this could happen here. I will personally deliver the evidence to you as soon as I can.'

Taking the box from the young police officer, who had just finished collating and labelling everything carefully, he left to go and face the music. *'You won't last five bloody minutes where they'll send you Robbie,'* he said to himself, as he left the car park.

Sarah was sat rocking Lily on the floor, while she started to try and comprehend what had happened. Feeling overwhelmed and just wanting to curl up in the corner and cry, she knew this wasn't an option right now as Lily needed her. Picking up the phone, she prayed that just for once Brian would answer. Three rings and it was picked up. But a young female voice answered sounding like she had just been woken up. 'Yeah, who is this?' a sleepy voice murmured.

'I need to speak to Brian, urgently!' Sarah said firmly, trying not to think about who this person could be.

'Well you'll have to wait a few minutes, he's in the shower,' she was told by someone now yawning.

Quickly putting Lily on her play mat, Sarah ran into the downstairs loo, shut the door and screamed 'Get my bloody husband now!'

'Sarah is that you? Whatever is the matter?' Brian answered quickly, slightly out of breath.

'Brian, you must come home. Last night I was raped in our garden, and I don't know what to do, please you have got to help me!' she cried down the phone, falling onto the cloakroom floor.

'Have you been to the police?' he asked, quite calmly.

'Of course I have. I had to have the most horrendous internal examinations to take evidence, and it was all on tape too from the security I had put in. They said they will get him probably in the next couple of days,' she explained, trying to breath between the tears.

'Well, there doesn't seem much point in me coming back then does there, as he won't be around in a few days and you can carry on, get back to normal. I'm sure this is very rare in such a small place, you wouldn't be that unlucky for it to happen again,' he said very matter of factly.

'What?! But Brian did you not hear me, I have been attacked - raped!'

'Poor you, that is awful Sarah, but I'm pretty busy right now. I'll try and get back in a couple of weeks, see if someone can cover my flights. You can't just swap them willy-nilly you know!' he said, starting to sound a little cross now. 'I'm really shattered Sarah and with a lot of flight delays yesterday, ended up getting little sleep, so will call you in couple of days to see how you are, ok?!'

'Ok?!' she shouted completely aghast now, and with a temper rising out of nowhere. 'No, that is not bloody ok! Do you ever listen to yourself or think about anyone else?

Your wife has been raped and you will try and change shifts but are a bit tired?!' she said incredulously. 'And obviously the lack of sleep has nothing to do with flights, does it! Tell you what Brian, don't bother. Don't bother coming back or phoning, I have completely had it this time!' she shouted.

'And what's that supposed to mean?'

'Der! It means, stay wherever you are with your little floozy and just give me an address to send some mail. Don't bother phoning either!' she shouted.

'Oh Sarah, come on, I think you are overreacting a bit don't you. Have you been to the doctors yet to get those tablets I said about, really think you could do with them?'

She couldn't answer.

'Are you still there? Now don't be silly or do anything silly. Lily needs you and so does my Mum,' he said slightly alarmed.

'Lily will be fine, Margaret will be fine. I will take care of them as I always do. But that's it Brian. I just need an address for you, don't bother coming back again,' she replied, quite coldly and calmly now.

'Don't be silly Sarah. My address is our home of course, I have nowhere else,' he replied.

'Not anymore!' and she hung up. The phone rang and rang, so she put it on silent and went back to Lily. Wiping the tears from her face, and trying her best to avoid touching her black eye, she picked up Lily and went to make them both a drink. Sitting down next to her on the sofa, she looked at her smiling and said 'Just me, you and lovely grandma now my gorgeous little girl,' and the floodgates opened again. Luckily Teletubbies suddenly appeared on the TV screen, and that was Lily transfixed for the next short while.

Sarah didn't want to be the gossip of the village, so decided it would be best to stay at home for the next week or so. Her swollen black eye would then have gone down and could hopefully be expertly covered with concealer, and she would really try and work on stopping herself from just suddenly bursting into tears too. The police had phoned to confirm everything had been submitted and they would keep her up to date with progress regularly. Incredibly, they hadn't arrested him yet, as there were some final details that needed processing before this could happen. They explained that everything needed to be captured properly to ensure success of conviction.

She phoned the care home and told them she wasn't very well and didn't want to pass anything onto Margaret or anyone else there, so would phone and speak to her later on in the week.

With the return of Will, Simon and all the stuff, life at the care home was particularly busy with lots of distractions and room transformations. By the end of the week, Betty was now sat at a good old fashioned bus stop, which she absolutely loved and began telling everyone about the bus she used to get to school every day. Others would also come and join her too and no residents attempted to leave the home any more, they would all just take a seat on the bench, 'happy as Larry'. The room was transformed into a time from the past, where everyone liked to return to in their minds. The items from the cupboard were setup in the corner, with a couple of small sofas, and it was like a living room from war time. Anyone that was feeling a bit distressed or agitated would make a beeline for it and the calmness would blanket them almost immediately. It was their safe space.

Margaret also appreciated all the changes, chatting to Will again about meeting Ron for the umpteenth time and having a little dance. All the staff were delighted and thanked Will for all his hard work, Simon too for enabling this to happen. Mind you, Will still had quite a long list of jobs to do before he could finally say goodbye and return home.

Noticing that Sarah and Lily had been absent for a few days, he just mentioned in passing to Simon that he hadn't seen them with Margaret this week. Hearing that she was poorly, he decided that chocolate cake always helped, no matter how ill you were. So popping into the local shop at the end of the day, he picked one up and headed up to her house, before taking his usual seat at the pub.

'Gosh, it was definitely an impressive house; she and her husband must be loaded!' he thought as he arrived at the entrance. Ringing the bell, he waited outside whilst Sarah was frantically trying to think of an excuse not to answer the door. Looking at Will on the screen she could see that he had a chocolate cake in his hands, *'what a lovely thing to do'* she thought, and reluctantly opened the door on the chain. Peering out from behind the door, she said 'Oh hi Will, what brings you here?'

Will could immediately sense that something was wrong and she wasn't probably poorly at all. Sporting a huge black eye and looking liked she had been crying for days, he asked genuinely concerned 'Sarah, is everything alright? What's been happening?'

'Oh this!' she said, pointing at her eye, 'stupid me tripped on the stairs and caught it on the banister. It will be ok though, thanks for asking. Just been feeling a bit poorly this week, so keeping my distance from everyone,' she said, very unconvincingly.

'Is your husband here looking after you then?' he replied.

'No, he's away at the moment. Well most of the time actually, it's just me and Lily.'

'Oh ok, I brought you this. Thought it might cheer you up if you are feeling rough, I mean chocolate cake helps everything get better in my eyes,' he said, smiling at her.

And she wasn't sure whether it was someone genuinely showing some care for her or what, but the tears just arrived out of nowhere.

'Sarah, please open the door. Talk to me,' he replied, worried initially that maybe it was her husband hurting her, but if he was away it couldn't be him.

Sarah quietly slid open the chain and the door opened. She walked, carrying Lily, into the kitchen in silence and shutting the door behind him, Will followed. Putting the chocolate cake on the side, he walked up to her. 'What's been happening Sarah?'

She walked over to the TV and grabbing the Tubbies video and her blanket, popped Lily in her bouncer and pressed play. Walking back to Will, she wandered over to the fridge and pointed at the beer and wine, 'Which would you prefer?' she asked. 'Beer please,' he replied, and pouring herself a glass of wine she went and sat on one of the stools at the island, gently patting the one next to her for him to take seat, all the while tears streaming down her face.

He didn't know what made him do it, but he just got off the stool and put his arms around her. With her head resting on his chest, she quietly sobbed for a while. Holding her, he could just feel the depth of her crying and it made him feel so sad. She had to tell him what had happened.

With 'uh, oh' coming from the television and Lily in fits of giggles at this blue thing zooming across the screen, she finally took a deep breath and began to talk. Will just listened, sometimes that's all it needs although deep down he wanted to go and find whoever it was. But it wasn't about him and his feelings, and that wasn't going to help Sarah either.

'So have you heard from the police yet?' he asked, waiting for a long pause after she had finished telling him everything.

'The last I heard they think an arrest will be made tomorrow, should hear by lunchtime all being well.'

'Have they any idea who it is?'

'Didn't say. I hadn't seen him around before though, maybe I was just unlucky bumping into him at the park,' she replied.

'Oh so you had seen him before then?'

'Only earlier that day, was sat with another couple of lads on the bench. Talk about wrong place, wrong time, don't know what made me go to the park that day apart from treating Lily before tea,' she said, with the tears starting to flow again.

Passing her another tissue from the box, Will asked, 'Couldn't help but notice the security you have here. Did it capture what happened?'

'Yes thank god. I took it with me straight to the police which is how they know for certain who it is. Just need to find him apparently.'

'Well that's great, hopefully that part will be over tomorrow then. Just need to support and help you through this, don't we. I mean physically and mentally, I can't imagine how hard that must be,' he replied, and taking hold of her hands again gave her a massive hug. He couldn't believe that her husband wasn't coming back either, although suspecting he was having an affair, she didn't want to see him anyway. He gently kissed the top of her head, while she wrapped her arms around his waist, sobbing again into his chest.

Lily started playing up the moment the video had stopped, and as it was getting late Sarah said she would be fine now thanks but must get Lily ready for bed. Will cut them each a bit of chocolate cake, which Lily thought was a great idea! Sarah didn't, and looked at him saying, 'All that sugar, she won't be getting to sleep anytime soon, thank you Mr Charlick,' and for the first time since he got there, she smiled.

'Well as it's my fault, I had better help tire her out.' And laughing as she squidged the cake into her mouth covering most of her face, hands and hair at the same time, said he would help give her a bath! For the first time that week, Sarah ended up laughing out loud so much it hurt. Will arrived in the bathroom with another glass of wine for her, and then while she sat on the toilet sipping it, he took over sorting out the 'chocolate monster' aka Lily. Lily found Will absolutely hilarious; he was such fun and made her laugh so much, an absolute natural. He had to admit, he had the best time too. Drying her off, and then insisting nappies can't be that hard, it took quite a few attempts to get it right with 'Miss Wriggle Pants' trying to turn over and escape everyday two seconds. He managed the pyjamas a little easier and as Sarah went to pick her up, she put her arms up to Will deciding that maybe he could do bedtime too. Sarah set the room up and Will carried her in, cuddling her head into his shoulder and quietly talking to her about all the things he could see, he rocked her until she fell fast asleep, carefully placing her down in her cot and tucking her blanket over her.

Sarah just watched from the door, smiling. She hadn't met anyone quite as caring as Will. While she got on with everyone in the village, she hadn't made good friends with anyone, just keeping herself to herself. With Lily and Margaret keeping her incredibly busy, and living a bit out of the way, there hadn't seemed to be any chance yet.

'Beginner's luck I think,' Will said, beaming at her as they walked down the stairs into the lounge.

'Thank you,' said Sarah. 'I mean for everything, I feel very lucky to have met you. By the way, how is Margaret - is she ok? I've been worried about her and felt really bad about not being able to visit this week?'

'She is having a whale of a time at the moment. We have just finished the redecoration of the large room and kitted it out - she absolutely loves it! You'll have to come and see it, think you will love it too,' Will replied.

'I bet it's fantastic, can't wait to pop up. A few more days and the swelling and bruising should be easier to cover, then we will be straight up to see her and have a look,' Sarah said smiling, touching her bruised cheek. 'Anyway, gosh look at the time. You must be shattered, blimey only popped over to bring cake and look what you have got caught up in!' Luckily the wine had numbed a little and she was feeling a bit more relaxed.

'Tell you what. Don't know how you feel about it, but how about I go and grab a couple of bits and sleep on the sofa. Just until they have caught him, I'm sure you would sleep better too. It's important for your recovery and Lily,' Will offered.

'Honestly I'm sure I will be fine, you need your sleep too with all the work going on at the home.'

'That sofa looks more comfy than my bed at the B&B, it's massive. And actually I'm going to insist, I won't sleep until I know you are both ok and he has been arrested. Then I'll go back to the B&B. We don't need to tell anyone, if that's what you are worried about, and you can trust me,' he replied, smiling.

'Oh it's not that at all. Well if you're sure, that would be lovely. I'll get you a duvet and pillow from upstairs then,' and she quickly disappeared up the stairs. Whispering into the baby monitor, she said 'Got a spare toothbrush and toothpaste here and you can borrow my husband's shaver, if that's any good? Save you having to go back now.'

Passing him the bedding, Will smiled at her and said 'Thanks, that's great. Don't worry, I can sort myself out.' Sarah grabbed them both a glass of water and handing him his, she said 'Night then Will, and thank you,' and for the first time since it happened, she slept.

Arriving down the stairs with Lily on her hip, Will was already up, bed tidied into a pile and coffee pot on. Bacon was sizzling in the pan and Lily instantly put her arms up to him, for him to carry her instead of mum. She had never done that for her own dad.

Sarah finished making the coffee and bacon sandwiches, and grabbing Lily her bottle, they all sat on the carpet in the lounge. Looking out at the garden, Will could now see the extensive grounds they owned. With a large lawn and then steps down to a second larger lawn, before reaching the stream, it was like somewhere he imagined celebrities own. To the right was thick woodland, unfortunately while picturesque, it was also perfect to hide in. The floor to ceiling glass windows were beautiful and incredibly modern, however at night (with no blinds) you could easily be watched, completely unaware.

As they all began their day with the slight air of optimism, no-one could foresee the phone call that was about to be made. With Will busy working at the care home, having checked she was sure she was ok as he could always make an excuse to stay, the phone rang. Picking it up quickly to hear the good news, she couldn't believe what she was hearing. Apparently all the evidence boxed up had been contaminated and the tape was blank. The young officer, who had been in charge of collating all the information ready for submittal, had been suspended pending further investigation and they were very sorry. They would of course keep an eye out for the suspect, although it would be hard to charge anyone without physical evidence. They had put an e-fit together of what they remembered from the footage, if she could pop in to have a quick look to confirm their description when she was able to. Silence. 'We are truly sorry about this,' said the policemen again, 'are you ok Sarah?'

'Fine,' she replied and hung up.

Will had already decided that as well as popping in to see them every day, he would take both Sarah and Lily out somewhere nice when this was all over. He knew the physical and emotional healing for her would take ages but wanted her to know he would always help in any way possible. He had grown very fond of them both, feelings he hadn't felt before.

Ringing the bell, he arrived at about 6.00pm to find Sarah busily wiping the tea off Lily's face and the floor, and a few other places she had managed to spread it to. Custard was her favourite pudding! Seeing the expression on Sarah's face unnerved him straight away.

'He hasn't been back has he?' he asked, alarmed at the difference in her since he had left that morning.

'No, but I got the call. You know I just can't believe it. All I'm going through and have been through, and they have lost everything! All they needed to do was their job, and they couldn't do it. The swabs, knickers, tape, photos, everything – all contaminated or blank. The young officer in charge of looking after the evidence has been suspended but apart from that, all they can do is a bloody e-fit which they want me to go and check. I mean, for god's sake, e-fits are useless as always end up looking like someone from that stupid misfits game! They don't ever look human! I was banking on them finding him so I could start to try and move on, and stop twitching at every noise I hear. I can barely face being in my own garden, it's not fair on me, Lily or the bloody dog. He is having to poo on a lead out the front, as I am too scared to go and find him at the bottom of the garden!' she said, beginning to cry.

Picking Lily up as she was starting to get very fidgety in her chair, Will put his arm around Sarah, pulling her close. 'Right, come on. You can quickly stay in the car while I grab my stuff at the B&B, but I'm definitely staying here to take care of you both and no, you can't say no or think about it either. I will be here until this is over, ok. Then you can kick me out! I know the village is full of gossips so if anyone asks, we shall say I am working on your loft conversion in the evenings.'

'Are you sure? I'll drive if you like as Lily's car seat is already in the car?'

'Great let's go,' he replied smiling.

On the way back she said it was silly with two spare bedrooms upstairs for Will to sleep in the lounge, so he moved into the one with the en-suite. Blimey, it was like being in a five star hotel!

The next morning Will phoned Simon to say he would be in slightly late today, and went with Sarah and Lily to the police station. Oh good god! The e-fit was shocking. 'Did you just ask a five year old to draw a picture of Robin from Batman and Robin?' Sarah snapped, furious with them. 'Are you taking the piss and not taking this seriously or something, or are you just hugely incompetent?! I mean, you have already proved the latter, losing all of the evidence!' she said, suddenly feeling very angry. 'I mean, no-one in the bloody world looks like that for crying out loud! Who runs this place? I need to see them now!' Blimey, she hadn't felt like she had this much strength in ages.

With that, Mr Gibbons, head of the police station and Robbie's dad appeared.

'Good morning Mrs Stephens. May I begin by saying how terribly sorry I am for everything that has happened. Please let me inform you that it has been dealt with and the officer concerned disciplined. We are all in shock and want to reassure you that we are doing everything we can to rectify the situation and find whoever is responsible.'

'Bullshit. And I'm sorry I wouldn't normally speak like this, but I don't think any of you have any idea of the trauma I'm going through. Does anyone actually care?! So to just respond with a ridiculous e-fit picture, which if it looked remotely like a human looks nothing like him anyway, I do wonder how any of you are employed to keep the public safe. I mean you can't even look after a pair of bloody knickers and a tape!' she exclaimed, bursting into tears. 'Don't any of you even remember seeing the tape? Look at the teeth for god's sake. You could see his are tobacco stained and rotten, these are like something from a goddamn toothpaste advert! Come on Will, let's not waste our time here!' and she stomped off out of the door. She hadn't notice the expression on Will's face had dramatically changed.

As they got in the car, Will passed her a tissue from the glove box. 'I'm so sorry Sarah,' he said.

'It's not your fault Will, is it?' she replied, trying to breath between the sobbing. Not wanting any of this to affect Lily, she quickly pressed play on the cassette player and Lily's favourite songs blasted out of the speakers, much to her delight.

'I spend quite a lot of time in and around the area, would you be able to tell me what he looks like?' asked Will gingerly.

'I can, but you're not Columbo or Bergerac, Will. You've got enough on your plate without having to turn detective too,' and she gave as good as description as she could. Will had all his suspicions confirmed after the teeth comment, and now knew there was no question it was Robbie. And the poor police officer, who was being used as a scapegoat and would probably lose his job and never work for the police again, was definitely being shafted by Robbie's dad. Filled with rage, he was tempted to go out looking for him straight away or letting the guys at the pub in on what was going on. But it had to be about Sarah and how she wanted things to happen.

'You ok?' she asked suddenly, noticing his change in mood.

'Yeah, just mad with the police really. Feel like going and finding him myself.'

'And if you hurt him and get arrested, how would that help me? I have to be honest with you Will and hope you feel the same, but I really like having you around with us. I can definitely speak for Lily too. So if you find out who it is and hurt him, you would be put in prison, no matter how much I would like you to do it! Then me and Lily would spend most of our week visiting either Grandma in the care home, whose marbles are diminishing on a weekly basis sadly, or you in prison! I mean, that would be completely shit as we would still be on our own,' she replied, smiling at him.

Blushing slightly, he replied 'Pleased you said that, hoping you would too. I'm loving spending time with you both, you have no idea how much. But I also know that you are married and will always respect that, so just friends,' he said, smiling back at her.

'Well I also need to look at dealing with that too. There's so much going on at the moment, so when hopefully this is all over I will be getting in touch with our solicitor. You have helped restore my anti-doormat mode and Brian needs to know that it's not ok to treat me like shit and still expect me to be here. I mean, it's times like this that you really find out who is there for you and people's true feelings don't you,' she replied, pulling back into their drive.

'*If only there had been a backup tape,*' thought Will to himself and decided he would be installing some additional discreet security. While Lily was having a nappy change, he popped out into the garden with the dog. As Sarah was finding this so incredibly hard, he had offered to sort out the dog walks and toilet runs for her, which she was only too pleased to accept. There were many large filled plant pots around the patio area on the top lawn, and some by the steps down to the second lawn too, which proved incredibly helpful. He of course hoped not to need it but installed a camera quickly just in case.

Talk around the village was that Robbie had gone back to live with his mum for a bit - she had really missed him and he had missed the city life. Truth be told, his dad had gone completely ballistic on viewing the evidence and sent him away to another town for the next few weeks, just until things died down.

Will kept an eye out for him of course, but just occasionally saw the other two. Without Robbie, they laid low, rarely popping into the pub and when they did, had little to say. Money on the pool table was left and turns taken. He was also growing closer and closer to Sarah and Lily every day; Simon had noticed the change in him too. 'You can tell me to mind my own business, but you seem even happier than usual. Nothing to do with a lovely young mum and her daughter by any chance is it? She deserves somebody just like you Will, not that idiot Brian who we all knew was having a fling with one of the girls in the village. Couldn't tell her though, not our place to say and really didn't want to see her get hurt. Margaret completely adores her and I hate to think what would have happened to her, if Sarah hadn't been around,' Simon said quietly, handing him a cup of tea.

'We've become good friends - that's all I can say,' Will replied smiling back at him, going a light pink colour.

With the police saying the case would be left open, but with no further leads there was little they could do at the moment, Sarah tried her best to start coming to terms with what had happened and move forward the best she could. Will certainly helped her feel relaxed and they had lots of laughs too, which really lightened the load.

Whilst she had so little control over the police situation, she could however take control over another area of her life that needed addressing.

Answering the phone on the fourth ring, Mr Madders listened to Sarah's marriage woes and agreed to a meeting to discuss the legalities the next week. Knowing her for some time now and having dealt with the family's legal matters, he wondered how Brian had been so lucky. Whilst Brian often came across as an arrogant twit, Sarah was just delightful and so caring. All of Margaret's care and changes in circumstance had come as a result of Sarah, not Brian. He rarely turned up to the meetings and when he did, showed little interest. Lots of sighing, and '*we must be nearly done aren't we? Does it really matter that much, she won't have a clue what's going on soon anyway,*' bolting out the door the minute he could. It did make him wonder what she saw in him. Sarah had also decided that she wouldn't mention what had happened to her, not unless she had to.

The following week, Will took some time off and the three of them drove to the main town for Sarah to meet Mr Madders. As they walked towards the solicitor's office, a man came out of a shop two doors down, nearly bumping into them. Instantly recognising Sarah from the photos, he quickly muttered 'I'm really sorry about your evidence, please know I didn't do anything wrong. I was so meticulously careful to place everything inside the box and seal it; there was no way anything could have changed by the time it got to the main police station.'

'Are you the officer that has been suspended?' she asked.

'Yes, doesn't matter about me. I didn't view the tape but a couple of the others did. I saw your photos though, that's how I recognised you. I would never say anything to anyone, but just wanted to say something happened to it, and it was nothing to do with me,' he replied quietly, looking down at the floor and hastily walked away.

'You need to park it for now Sarah. Concentrate on Mr Madders and then we'll have a think later about the police,' said Will, giving her a quick hug and pushing Lily off to see the ducks at the pond.

Mr Madders was as always completely charming, and unlike the local police, highly competent and effective. She would be in a much better position if she could prove adultery and therefore the blame could be completely parked at Brian's door, no question. Otherwise, there were other options available. And lovely, dear Margaret...

Apparently when she sold her house and moved in with them, she already had concerns about Brian's behaviour. She could see the selfishness and had heard some things about his out of house activities that she wished she hadn't. Completely adoring Sarah, she had purchased an insurance policy to cover any future care home costs, should she get the dreaded dementia that her late mother had, and had left the rest to her. She left a note with Mr Madders for her, should the situation ever arise. Sarah couldn't believe it and felt so touched and emotional. Handing her the letter, he said 'Read this when you get home. She always wanted to know that you were ok, said you were sent from the angels. You were only to have this if she couldn't give it to you herself, and if you were in trouble or your marriage was breaking down. So take care and I will be in touch about everything else.'

Sarah walked out of the office onto the high street pinching herself. Checking the letter was still in her handbag, and she wasn't imagining it, she went to find

Will and Lily. Seeing them in the distance, she smiled so hard her cheeks hurt. Will was squat down with Lily on his lap, surrounded by ducks wanting their bread. Lily was giggling and attempting to throw it as far as she could, which of course wasn't very far. Will was breaking off pieces and passing them to her, so they didn't get to choke on the whole slice. It was so adorably cute.

Coming up behind them, Will turned to see her stood watching. Grinning, he said 'Want a go?' and getting closer, passed her a slice of bread. As she crouched down next to him, he said 'Did it go well?'

'Better than expected,' she replied smiling, and squeezed his hand.

The rest of the day was all about having fun with Lily. By bedtime, she was completely shattered and fell asleep the minute her head touched the pillow. Sitting on the stools at the island in the kitchen, Will opened the bottle of wine and poured them both a glass. Sarah pulled her bag up off the floor, took the letter out and started reading.

'My dearest Sarah,

If you are reading this, it means that bloody awful dementia disease has messed my brain up too, just like my dear mum. I might now not be able to say exactly what I would want to, so that is why I am writing this letter.

After losing my mum and my dear Ron in such a short space of time, I never thought I would be able to cope with life or ever enjoy it again. But you changed that for me, for which I am forever grateful. The day Brian brought you home to meet us for the first time I knew instantly you were special. We don't always know why, we just get this feeling and our instincts are usually right. That evening when you said goodbye to go home, Ron and I both looked at each other, goosebumps on our arms and said 'If he ever lets that one out of his arms, he's a bloody idiot!'

You raise your children in the best way you know how, but after that it is up to them. I love Brian, he is my son. I do not love though his selfishness and behaviour at times, we didn't raise him to be like that. I have been concerned sometimes at the way he has treated you, you do not deserve it. So if Mr Madders has passed you this letter, it is because you are now having to look at venturing out on your own, as you cannot stay with Brian any longer. Know that me and Ron would both support you in this decision if we were around to be able to, and you have our blessing.

Brian is an adult now and must make his way through life and be accountable for his decisions, good and bad. He will always be financially secure, so this is just for you.

I wish you all the very best in the world Sarah and I hope you find true love one day; it is the least you deserve. If this helps you just a little bit, know it will make me the happiest person in the world,

We feel blessed to have had you in our lives, and until we meet again somewhere else (hopefully),

All our love and blessings,

Margaret (and Ron) xx'

With tears streaming down her face, there were no words. A cheque was enclosed for £250,000. They just sat in silence for the next few minutes, taking it all in. 'Can you believe it?' said Sarah, quietly. 'No-one has ever done anything like that for me or said such beautiful, heartfelt words. Things like this don't happen to people like me; well not unless it's in the movies.'

'What do you mean people like you, I don't think you realise yourself how special you are,' said Will.

Getting up to get them each another drink, Sarah began talking about her life in care. Taken away from her alcoholic parents at the age of five, she had grown up being passed from foster family to foster family, before moving into a permanent children's home at nine years old. She hated it, always felt everyone was there because it was just a job, no-one really cared - they were just paid to be there. You were watered and fed but that was about it. So the minute she was sixteen she left and vowed to try and change her life. Answering an advert in the local newspaper, she got an interview with an airline and luckily was accepted to train as an air hostess. She absolutely loved it, meeting everyone and pretending everything was fine whilst travelling the world. It suited her down to the ground, and of course a few years later that is how she met Brian. He already had a bit of a reputation, while the cats away and all that. But people could change, that's what she hoped. Maybe he just hadn't found the right person yet and just maybe that could be her. He was handsome and completely charming, with lots of money too to wine and dine you anywhere in the world. Although he was eight years older than her, had been married before and only for a year, she really felt he was the one. How wrong she was, but would never regret it because she had Margaret and Lily in her life. Margaret had always been like a mum to her, the one she would have loved to have had and so when she was finding things tough, it was an absolute pleasure to have her move in with them. Brian was away often anyway or working long days, so they had time on their own and grew very close. Lily arriving was the icing on the cake, but that also showed up the massive cracks in her relationship with Brian. 'And the rest you know,' she said, smiling at the memories that were triggered from talking about Margaret and Lily.

She then changed tack. 'Blimey must be the wine making me talk so much, not just the letter. Anyway, Mr Mysterious Will, I really don't know lots about you and how you have ended up at Green Meadows. So what's your story?'

Will for the first time felt so comfortable with someone, apart from Alf, that he began to tell his story. Missing out some of the video camera parts, he talked for what seemed like ages while Sarah listened attentively.

'Bloody hell, you haven't had it easy either have you!' she said at the end, and feeling slightly merry from the wine, got off her stool and kissed him. It just felt right and if he didn't look happy about it or pulled away, she would apologise and blame the wine and what was going on. But he didn't pull away.

'But until everything is finalised with Brian, we both know it can go no further don't we. We'll just have to wait and will know for sure then that it is definitely right. I don't want it to be just a rebound thing,' said Will.

Kissing him again and then pulling away, Sarah said 'You are so definitely not a rebound thing! I can guarantee that I will be waiting until it's all over and just hope you are too.'

'Oh that's not up for negotiation, I will guaranteed be here,' Will said, and went off to walk the dog in the garden and get some fresh air, before he could get carried away.

He saw the light go on upstairs in Sarah's room, so guessed she must have decided to go up for some reason. Grabbing the dog, he wandered back up to the house, locked the doors and turned out the lights. Standing on the landing, he called out quietly 'Night then,' and Sarah's door opened slightly. 'Night Will, see you in the morning,' she said smiling, and closed the door again. '*Way too tempting*,' she told herself and got in to bed. Lily was quietly snoring and she fell asleep almost instantly.

Crouching down completely still, Robbie squatted in the woods looking up at the house. '*Bloody video cameras, who the hell can afford them? Won't be able to record anything this time, silly bitch! Causing me all this trouble with my dad, I've never seen him so angry. I warned you not to tell anyone, you are properly going to get it this time!*' he muttered to himself, smoking a joint, watching.

He'd seen her shut her blinds upstairs and the light go out. Kicking himself for arriving a bit late, he decided to wait and see if she would come back down for any reason. If not, he would bide his time until an opportunity arose and come back each evening. Fortunately he hadn't spotted that there was anyone else staying there, Will's bedroom was at the front of the house.

After about an hour he gave up, deciding he would come back tomorrow.

The next morning, Lily was delighted to see Will first thing and insisted he gave her breakfast. Sarah passed him his cup of tea and toast, reassuring him that they would be fine thanks and look forward to seeing him later. Waving him off, they began their normal day's activities. While Lily caught up on the latest episode of Tubbies, Sarah checked the cameras. '*Nothing - great,*' she said to herself, and instantly felt more relaxed. They had a lovely day that was made all the better, when the doorbell went and Will returned. Arms straight up, Lily got in for a cuddle first.

While Sarah cooked them some food, Will insisted he would get Lily ready for bed. After her bath, he took her downstairs to say goodnight to her mum. 'Blimey I could get used to this,' said Sarah smiling, giving Lily a kiss goodnight. Like the night before, he turned the main lights off, put on the little nightlight and cuddling her into his chest, gently rocked and talked to her with a hushed voice.

There in the woods, same as the night before, Robbie was back again. He'd found an old spade by an outbuilding on the edge of the woods and thought it could come in handy. Seeing Sarah through the glass windows, he grinned. Perfect. Quietly approaching each of the cameras, and having covered the spade with an old bit of cloth he'd found to quieten the noise, he smashed both rear cameras effortlessly. Chucking the rest of his joint on the floor, he crept up nearer to the house. *'The great thing about these massive posh windows at night, is that I can see in but you can't see out,'* he thought to himself, *'should have put up bloody blinds or something if you want some proper privacy.'*

Sitting watching on the steps between the lawns, he knew it would only be a matter of time before the dog needed to have a wee. *'Must be patient,'* he said to himself. He was starting to get a bit irritated at how long he was having to wait, so rolled and lit another joint. *'Come on you silly bitch. In there, stirring your poncey pot, smiling away. Well you won't be bloody smiling soon. Told you I would do something if you told anyone about before. Won't have cameras recording us this time to grass me up, getting me in shit with my dad too. Not just a black eye, you'll be unrecognisable when I have finished,'* he said to himself, sneering.

Lily had finally fallen asleep, and gently laying her down in her cot, Will quietly closed her door to go downstairs. Glancing at the security camera screens as he walked past, he suddenly stopped, seeing that only one screen was working, the one for the front. Creeping back up to Lily, waking her up at which she let out a wail, he went out onto the landing. 'Sarah, my arms are nearly going to fall off and I'm busting for a wee too. Any chance we could swap for five?' he called out.

''Course, no problem. Wait a sec, I'll just turn this off and be up.'

Passing Lily over and discreetly ushering them into her bedroom to not rouse any suspicion that something might be up, he said, 'Tell you what, when you've got her back down, why don't you have a nice relaxing bath, as it's still quite early yet. I'll finish the dinner, get us a glass of something and quickly get some paperwork I should have already done out of the way. Then we can chill in front of the TV together for a bit.'

'You sure? That sounds perfect,' she replied.

'Absolutely, see you in a bit,' he replied, and found the light switch for the downstairs. Turning the lights off, he headed for the front door. *'Probably nothing, just me overreacting but just in case,'* he said to himself, quietly closing the door behind him.

'Oh for fuck's sake, where's she gone now? Let's hope it's just to sort out the brat and then she'll be back down. Calm down Robbie, good things come to those that wait!' he muttered.

Creeping quietly around the cars at the front, Will nearly tripped on an old piece of twine. *'Jesus Christ!'* he exclaimed quietly, picking it up and stuffing it in his pocket with his heart now racing.

Coming around the side, he thought he spotted a slight movement near the steps, so tread very carefully, desperately trying not to make a sound. Squinting in the darkness, a puff of smoke drifted off by the steps and the smell was unmistakeable. Will wasn't sure what it was, as had never been violent or in a fight in his life, but having experienced extensive bullying in school and seen what some people seem to get away with, spotting Robbie with a spade in hand, knew it was finally time for payback. For all the bullies that get away with it, with excuses of their problems at home, the rage he felt was extreme. There was never an excuse, we choose our actions and therefore must be accountable for them too! Robbie had no idea anyone was there, until the spade was ripped out of his hand and smashed against the back of his head. Instantly falling forward, Will couldn't help but land another blow. He wasn't sure what he was going to do next, but knew Robbie needed to be out of it, to give him time to think.

Quickly tying his hands behind his back with the twine, and saying *'you little shit, this one is from Sarah!'* struck him for the third time. Luckily Robbie wasn't a big guy, so easy for Will to pick up and chuck him over his shoulder. 'Bloody hell, what shall I do with him now?' he muttered to himself. Throwing him in the boot of his car, he popped back into the house. 'Sarah, I'm just popping out to get us some wine, ok! Back in a mo,' and left before he could hear the answer. Driving speedily down the lanes, he decided to dump him outside the police station with a note, praying that no-one was around. In the pitch black, he parked up around the corner and quickly carried him to the door, dumping him on the floor. Will scribbled a note on a scrap piece of paper in the car and stuck it with masking tape to his forehead, it just said *'think you might be looking for me, haven't seen a toothbrush for a while!*' He then ran over to the phone box and dialled the station, said he'd heard some commotion in the car park and hung up. He watched as they opened the door to find Robbie.

Trying to catch his breath, he strolled over to the shop and bought a special bottle of wine.

Getting in the door, Sarah was smelling and looking as gorgeous as ever, her eyes twinkling and light music playing in the background. 'Everything ok? Good choice of wine by the way,' she asked. Taking her in his arms, he kissed her gently and said, 'Yes fine, come on I'm starving!'

Taking the dog out for his night-time wee, he dug around in the plant pot, fishing out the tape. The last bit would need cutting out, but hoped it would have picked up Robbie, at least to ask the question of why he was there hiding outside the house and had smashed the cameras. He phoned Alf, and whilst explaining that he would update him on all the goings-on shortly, asked him if he could help with a bit of editing. Alf agreed straight away and they arranged to meet up early the next morning at a service station, half way between them.

Sneaking out of the house at 4.30am, Will was so pleased to see Alf. And while Alf got busy with the tape, Will began telling him about the past few weeks. 'Poor girl,' said Alf, 'and by the look on your face you aren't just going to help and walk away, look completely smitten if you ask me,' he said smiling, delighted that Will had finally met someone special.

'I can't wait for you to meet her Alf, and little Lily!' said Will, excitedly.

'Hang on a minute, sssh. Listen to this,' Alf said. As well as showing Robbie in full view, the tape had recorded all of his mutterings on the steps, clear as day. A few minutes later, 'Whoa, didn't know you hadn't it in you. Bloody hell, cracking shot!' Alf said, as he saw the spade land and Robbie drop like a sack of spuds. He agreed to make two copies of the tape, editing it in the right place, and would post them to the two police stations from their local post office back at home. Giving each other a hug, they arranged for Alf and Max to come and visit the following week, if everything had died down. Alf would keep the original with all the others.

Getting back to Sarah's, he snuck back in, quietly closing the door. Hearing Lily starting to wail, he quickly put on the kettle and got her bottle ready. Half asleep, Sarah appeared on the stairs with Lily on her hip. 'Didn't hear you get up?' she said.

'Got lots on today so thought I'd make an early start. Here you are,' he said passing Lily's bottle and going back to make them both a drink.

While she sat on the sofa and fed Lily, he made the tea and toast and then joined them.

Looking out across the lawns to the woods made him shudder slightly, thinking about who was sat there watching the night before. He didn't know what made him say it, but said 'Do you think you'll want to live here forever?'

'Oh god no! I never wanted this house in the first place; it was Brian who insisted it was perfect. To be honest, I can't wait to start looking for somewhere else. I need to be around here for Margaret, but there are quite a few villages around here and now she has given me this money, I don't need to wait for the divorce to be finalised and sell this place. I don't want anything from Brian anyway, he can keep this house,' she replied.

'What about you? Will you go back to your home when you have finished at the care home?' she asked, not sure she wanted to hear the answer.

'Well, it depends if there are any other offers? I would happily leave my house if there was another option. But like you, need to be near Alf. I also promised I would carry on looking after the other care home too, Angie made me promise,' he said.

'Well, before we decide anything, would you come and view some houses with me and Lily?'

'Would love to, I've got this Saturday off if you can arrange anything by then?' said Will.

'Great, I will pop into the estate agents in the main town today and see what I can organise,' she answered, suddenly getting a bit excited about the days to come. Being able to take back control, thanks to dear Margaret, had suddenly given her a positive feeling about the future.

With concealer covering her recent trauma, she and Lily spent the morning wandering in and out of the local estate agents in the town. With an armful of property details, she sat in the coffee shop sorting them into 'yes,' 'maybe' and 'absolutely not' piles, while Lily played in her highchair with her new Teletubbies pretend TV.

And while Will was busy working out where the *'god awful stench'* was coming from in Betty's bedroom, Alf was at the post office counter sending two envelopes by first class post, guaranteed delivery.

Having woken up in his dad's office, not really understanding how he had got there, Robbie was feeling the wrath of his dad.

'How the hell did I produce such a dimwit bloody idiot of a son? I spent a bloody fortune on that hotel and all you had to do was stay there until everything died down! The officers are already suspicious, and the ones that had seen the tape I've had to pay off. Let's hope whoever hit you knocked some bloody sense into you!' he screamed in his face. 'You can stay with me until I know you are ok and then get your arse back to that hotel.'

Robbie had no recollection of what happened. *'One minute I was sat in the dark waiting, the next I woke up here at the police station,'* was all he could say.

While Lily was having her afternoon nap, and having sorted a shortlist of properties to show Will later, Sarah decided to give the police station a quick call to see if there had been any progress with her case.

Slighting fumbling over his words, the officer that answered the phone informed her that they were still looking for the attacker but no leads as yet. The e-fit had been circulated in the area but there hadn't been any response. 'I mean really?! Are you surprised? It doesn't look like anyone does it! I would like to speak to the most senior policeman there please, as I need someone to take this seriously. That picture needs changing for a start, I can't believe anyone authorised it to be released!' she shouted down the phone.

'Madam, our police chief is the only person who is able to authorise releases of these pictures for circulation. He actually made some changes before its release as he didn't feel happy with the accuracy of the one we had produced,' she was informed.

'Is there something wrong with his sight? Oh don't bother, to be honest I don't know why I called!' and she hung up.

Updating Will over dinner of her phone call, he was also surprised that nothing had changed after their most recent arrival at the station. '*Still tomorrow's post should do it,*' he thought to himself. Listening to Sarah having a massive rant and then collapsing into floods of tears again, things had better change tomorrow. Will also reassured her that whilst the rear cameras weren't working, he had it all in hand so not to worry. They decided to leave looking at property details to the next evening, as they weren't really in the mood for it now.

Robbie was recovering at home, lying low for now. Whilst the hotel was still booked out for him, his dad had insisted on keeping an eye on him in case he had concussion. Going to the hospital would be a bad idea, unless he took a turn for the worse. It would be best to try and just rest at home, where no questions would be asked. His grandparents were staying with them at the moment and this was proving to be a huge inconvenience to getting rid of the damning evidence his dad had stashed. The plan was to burn it, but they were always popping up out of nowhere asking questions, interested they would say in what was going on. So for now it had been hidden away with the other stuff.

By midday the next day, Robbie and his dad's worlds had changed dramatically. Wondering who the hell was thudding so heavily on the front door, he dragged himself off the sofa, getting there just before grandad. 'Just a fucking minute, no need to bang the door down!' Robbie shouted, approaching the door.

'Police, Robbie Gibbons you are under arrest!' and he was read his rights. Handcuffed and put in the back of the police car, he was taken away. His grandparents were horrified at what was happening, *'their dear Robbie'*. Saying little but showing them the warrant, a policeman took them into the kitchen to make them a cup of tea while the other officers started their search.

At the same time, two senior policemen arrived at the village police station to talk to Mr Gibbons. He had already seen the package that had arrived, and was cursing as to how bloody stupid his son was *'I mean, who talks to himself out loud, what a bloody idiot!'* Denying of course that he knew what Robbie was talking about on the tape, he started covering his back. His son was a regular drug taker and had only recently moved back with him, after his mum had asked him to leave; her influence seemed to have changed him for the worse. He was trying his best to teach him the error of his ways, but this was no small task. If he'd had any idea of what he'd done, of course he would have brought him in himself. Trying to make light of it, he explained he had suspended the officer in charge of the evidence and was almost certain that he would be found incompetent and lose his job. He had taken decisive action and had no idea why Robbie had mentioned him on the tape, probably too high to know what he was talking about. He started gently moving them towards the door as could now feel the sweat dripping down the back of his neck and desperately needed them to leave. Thanking them for taking the time to visit, he returned to his office without speaking to anyone, slumping down in his chair.

Pulling out of the car park, they both had their concerns as to what had been happening here but couldn't yet prove anything. With their radio crackling into action, they heard from the search team. In the garage at the family home they had found a box containing a tape, photo and some knickers. They were lifting fingerprints but were pretty sure who had put it there. There was also a substantial quantity of drugs and cash found nearby.

Ten minutes later, Mr Gibbons was being led out of the station and put in the back of their car. Only three years to retirement and with the money he had made, reselling the drugs that had been seized in raids, he would have been sunning it up in his home in Spain. Now that was never going to happen. Chances are they would start digging around further.

Viewing the tape at the main police station, no-one said anything for a few minutes after it had finished. Poor girl, and who would let their child get away with doing something like that!

DI Eleanor Price, one of their most senior detectives, phoned Sarah and asked her to come in. The call had come as a surprise to Sarah and she whisked Lily into her seat and set off for the police station. While Lily was avidly watching her Teletubbies TV in her pushchair, Eleanor explained as much as she could. A man called Robbie Gibbons had been arrested and they were sure it was him. He was of course denying it or saying *'no comment'* to every question but the evidence that had come to light was conclusive - he would be charged. If Sarah could pick him out on a line-up, that would be really helpful for the case too, although they could understand if she didn't want to. The glass was one way, so he would be unable to see her.

As the five men started walking in, she instantly looked at DI Price and said 'Number four, it's definitely him.'

DI Price smiled and thanked her. 'Hope this can give you some closure now. I know it can't change what you have been through, but at least to know that he will be put away for many years to come, I really hope this can help begin your healing,' she said, shaking her hand and then giving her a quick hug. 'I am truly sorry for what has happened up to now, but please be reassured that we are dealing with this now and there will be at least one conviction.' She couldn't say any more about who else might have been involved.

'What about that young officer though, you know the one who was suspended?' Sarah asked.

'There are a few things other things that I can't comment on but are being dealt with and I can reassure you though, that he will be back at work soon.'

'Thank you,' said Sarah, and she really meant it. Yes, she was right that this didn't suddenly make everything ok and back to normal now, but being able to walk out in the garden without worrying who might be there would be a start.

Racing home, she got in the house and cuddling Lily they did a little dance around the kitchen. The dog started barking so she opened the doors and wandering out onto the lawn, she felt ok for the first time since it happened. The feelings weren't completely gone and the area where she had been attacked was still out of bounds for her. But luckily with it being such a huge garden, she didn't need to go over there. She would also be moving on soon, in more ways than one.

Brian had phoned and left a couple of messages, checking she wasn't still being silly and had calmed down now. He was hoping to be home in about three weeks, so hoped she would have seen the doctor by then and be feeling, and more importantly acting, more normal now. He also hoped she would call him back to let him know his mum was ok too. Pressing the delete button instantly, she had no intentions of returning his calls.

Will arrived while Lily was having her tea, who was then insistent that Will do the spoon and refused to open her mouth until this happened. Dumping his stuff on the floor and taking the spoon to shovel in the next mouthful, he said 'So how was your day?' Sarah told him everything that had happened - the best news in a while! Will smiled and listened, whilst making sure he kept up with the pace of Lily's feeding requirements. Everything he had hoped for her had happened.

Once Lily was in bed, Will then thought he had better mention and remind each other of the terms of his stay, '*I will be here until they find and arrest him.*' 'You must be feeling so relieved though. You know he will be in prison for years to come, so at least you don't have to worry about him coming back.'

'You know, it is a massive relief. Every twig snapping was making me panic and I was always on edge, scared that he would come back. I don't know how I would have coped without you, I mean that,' she replied.

'Well for me, it has been an absolute pleasure and I really mean that. I have loved every minute with you and Lily, and can't wait to get back here after work. But I also remember that we agreed I would be here until they found him, then should leave,' he said.

'But I think that may have changed a bit, well for me it has,' she said, smiling at him, hoping to god he agreed.

'Me too. So what does this mean?' he replied, smiling at her.

'Well, I forgot to tell you but Mr Madders has been doing some digging and asking around. Turns out *Madam* that answered the phone, isn't his first, the lying git!

Couple of girls in the village too, can you believe it?! So with divorce on grounds of adultery, me and Lily are entitled to at least half of everything here. I told him I don't want any of it, just a fresh start, but I'd love you to be a part of it once the divorce has gone through.'

'Come here you, I'm kind of pinching myself right now, being with you and Lily is a dream come true for me,' he said, taking her in his arms and kissing her. 'Now let's start having a look at those properties shall we?' he said pulling away gently, knowing it would be too easy for things to go further.

After looking through them all and chatting way into the night, they both decided that it might be better for her to rent first and see where life took them. Neither of them knew the area that well, and both hoped Margaret had many years in her yet, so renting initially would be a better option and quicker too.

They arranged to view three properties on the Saturday and were both so excited, as they set off to see the first one. It was perfect: a chocolate box cottage, with a beautiful garden with lots of space for Lily and the dog to burn off some energy. Completely enclosed, next to four other cottages, it had the privacy she wanted but without the isolation. Phoning the agent the minute they left, and cancelling the other viewings, she just had that feeling that it was right. Also, as it was vacant, she could move-in in two weeks if that suited. 'That is perfect thank you, I will be over to sign all the paperwork in about an hour!' And they sped off to do just that.

The next two weeks flew past. Just packing the things that belonged to her and Lily, Will arranged to hire a van to help her move out. Simon offered the farmer's van much to their amusement. 'Depends when you hope to get there, as long as you are in no rush?!' he said, laughing.

'Kind offer, but will sort one out,' replied Will, smiling.

With concealer now covering up the remnants of the bruising, Sarah and Lily could at last visit Margaret. It had felt like a lifetime since she'd last seen her. Sarah kept saying to Margaret in the mirror when she was getting up each morning, *'not to go anywhere please, she would be there soon'*. Will was also desperate for Alf and Max to meet everyone, so arranged for them to come and see what he had been up to at the home at the same time.

Marvelling at his bus stop, Simon gave him a huge handshake as he was introduced to Alf. 'We can't thank you enough, can we Agnes?' as she arrived and parked her bum on the seat. Agnes always liked to be first in the queue if at all possible. Alf was delighted, saying it was Will's idea and he was only too happy to be able to help. Max bound around making friends with everyone, and as Margaret turned the corner to see Sarah and Lily coming through the door, she burst into tears.

'Are you well now Sarah, I have missed you so much?!' she exclaimed, giving her a massive hug.

'All good now thanks Margaret, we have really missed you too! We will never leave it that long again if we can help it,' she said, hugging her tightly. Amazed that for the first time in ages she had remembered her name too.

Margaret took her and Lily off to see all the changes and her new dancing area. Sitting with a couple of the residents in the new room, Sarah couldn't believe the transformation. *'He is just amazing, where did he come from?'* she muttered to herself, as she was then shown the sofa area that took you back many decades. Such a beautiful, calm space.

Alf then finally got his chance to meet the very lovely Sarah and Lily. '*With some people, you can just tell like me and my Elsie*' he thought to himself, on seeing Will and Sarah together. It was just right - perfect. It was something he had wished for Will for as long as he had known him. Sarah and Alf got on like a house on fire too from the off. Everything was just falling into place.

Strolling around the home gardens, Will finally got a chance to speak to Alf on his own. Alf had been his rock for all these years and he never wanted that to change. He had missed him and Max very much and was looking forward to returning home, but was worried about how Alf would see the future too. Will and Sarah had already agreed that he would just visit while she settles and the divorce goes through. All being well, if their relationship develops, they would think about buying somewhere together in the future, but wanted to take it slow for now.

Will also knew work at the care home would be finished in the next three weeks.

'When you find a good 'un Will, you mustn't let them go. Blimey I'm becoming a bit of an old codger now myself, so don't worry about me,' he said after hearing of his plans.

'But you have always been there for me and I would hope you would agree that I have for you too. I don't ever want you to think that I am leaving you, that will never be the case, as you mean too much.'

'That's really kind Will, but you can't put your life on hold for me, I wouldn't like that. Why don't you see how it goes and we can decide at the time what needs to happen. No-one knows the future, not even that Mystic Meg,' he replied, smiling.

Before they knew it, it was moving day. Brian had called to say he had managed to swap a flight, so would be able to come home for four days next week. He was getting a bit fed up with her not returning his calls but hoped she had seen the doctor for the depression tablets and maybe they were making her sleepy. He would need to be out for one evening when he got back but other than that, would be around so maybe she could organise a babysitter, *'Lily was surely old enough for that now.'*

'Oh my god, you are such an arse!' she shouted at the answer machine, listening to the message. 'Delete' and it was gone. Mr Madders hadn't been able to get hold of him so had sent the letter to their home, ready for his return. For the first time in a long time, rather than feeling upset, Sarah giggled as she thought about Brian's face when he opened the door. Packing the boxes was an absolute pleasure, with her now looking forward to the future.

Moving day arrived and they quickly packed up the van. Bundling the dog and Lily into the car, she said her final goodbyes to her old life and locked the door. *'Time to move on now.'* With Will following her in the van, she took a deep breath and set off to drop her house keys off with Mr Madders and collect the ones to her new life.

Opening the door to her new home, the sunshine flooded from the kitchen through the hall to greet them. What a welcome. With the dog on his lead and Lily in her arms, she wandered through to open the back door. Walking out onto their cottage lawn, fully enclosed by fencing she let both the dog and Lily go and explore. She hadn't felt this secure in a long time. Knowing they were both fine, with a stable door half closed she went back to the car to grab her stuff. Hearing squeals of laughter from Lily, they both walked through the kitchen to see the dog had found an old squeaky ball from somewhere and was now going completely crazy with it. Stood watching, they couldn't help but burst out laughing.

Will finished bringing in the boxes while Sarah sorted out Lily's cot. Being furnished had been a huge bonus as she had little to start with and putting her bedding on the bed, she collapsed onto it with a huge smile. Her tears were happy ones for a change, slightly overwhelmed but happy. Never thinking she would have the courage to take control like she had, she felt proud of herself, probably for the first time in her life.

With the boxes in, she and Lily quickly got back in the car and followed Will to take the van back. Popping into the chippy to get fish and chips to celebrate, they got back and all sat on a blanket in the garden, tucking into their food and sipping some bubbly that Will had brought with him. Lily insisted on feeding herself the chips and beans, with the occasional bit landing in her mouth and the rest everywhere else, including Will and Sarah. The dog sat patiently, praying he would get to have some too.

'Excuse me, excuse me, hello!' they heard someone calling out.

Sarah rushed up to the front door to find a lady standing there with a steaming hot apple crumble.

'Hi, my name is Kathy. I saw the van and you unpacking it, and just thought you might like this after such a busy exhausting day,' she said, handing her the baking dish wrapped in a tea towel and a small jug of custard.

'Oh my goodness that is so kind. My name is Sarah and this is my daughter Lily and my friend Will,' she said as they joined her to see what was going on.

'Well I won't keep you, but just wanted to say if you need anything just knock or bang on the wall,' she said, turning around to go back next door.

'Thank you and the same to you too, anything just give us a shout,' Sarah replied, smiling at her delightful new neighbour.

Closing the door, and with Lily trying to shove her fingers in the custard, she quickly dished it out and they took their bowls back out to the blanket. 'What a lovely thing to do,' she said, looking at Will.

'Yep, think you have found a good place here,' he replied, feeling relieved for her.

She settled in really quickly and found the drive to see Margaret so easy - very handy for Will too. Whilst waiting for the legalities of her divorce to be finalised, they had agreed that it was too tempting to stay over, particularly after a couple of drinks. So he had moved back into the B&B temporarily, spending the evenings with them and arriving there late each evening. Sarah gave herself a little pinch at how her life had changed more than she could ever have imagined, and so much for the best. The feeling of taking that control back from Brian, who on reflection she could now see had often treated her like shit and knocked her self-esteem and confidence to an all time low. But no more, thanks to Margaret and Will.

Brian arrived home a few days later and went completely crazy to find she and Lily had gone, just a letter from Mr Madders waiting for him. Shouting at the voicemail message he got every time she didn't answer, he demanded that she return to discuss this with him. Smiling as she listened to his despair, having being on the end of it herself so many times, she just pressed delete. Speaking with Mr Madders, he confirmed that he would be working particularly hard on her case to get it through the system as quickly as was feasibly possible, and would respond to Brian's message on her behalf. After one particularly fraught call from Brian, who was not going to be agreeing anything reasonable, he reassured Sarah that there was little to worry about.

Having got one of his junior staff to spend some time in the village finding out what she could, she came across one of the girls he had slept with. He apparently had never mentioned he was married, and when she found out about Sarah and confronted him with it, said they were about to get divorced as it wasn't working out. She felt very used as Brian had dumped her by leaving a message on her answer machine. '*Bastard didn't realise that in village life, everyone knows everyone else's business. Idiot city boy then went and tried it on with one of my friends*' was the response from her and she was only too happy to be cited in the legal paperwork.

Mr Madders had informed him that he would be required to pay maintenance for Lily and would also arrange for access to be put in place. Sarah dreaded this in some way, as he had never spent any time with Lily on his own, never even changed a nappy or made a bottle. Always too tired, and '*as I wasn't working why should he have to do it anyway! He was bringing in the money, wasn't that enough!*' was a regular rant at being asked to give her a hand.

She needn't have worried. Whilst Will fell over backwards to spend time with Lily, thoroughly loving every minute, Brian's flight schedule seemed to have got even busier. Arranging to take her to the park nearby for an hour on the following Saturday, as that was all he could manage at the moment, he of course didn't show. *'Apparently, there has been a last minute change and his flight brought forward, so didn't get chance to phone and cancel, sorry'* was the explanation left on the answer machine a week later. Mr Madders had made contact again with the girl from the village about some of the paperwork details, only to be told even more relevant news. 'She had seen him with a girl, on the Saturday he was supposed to be with Lily, at the pub at about 12 noon, getting completely pissed. And one of the regulars said they didn't leave until just before last orders at 10.50pm!' Mr Madders thanked her and made sure everything was noted in the file. As it turned out Brian had already decided not to contest the divorce, just hadn't told anyone yet. He had the house, money and a uniform that helped him so much in the bedroom department - *what was there to fight for?*

Will's work at the home was coming to an end - only about five days left he reckoned. He'd been in touch with Alf and arranged to be back at home the next week. Simon, all the staff and the residents were truly delighted with how the home had taken shape and had loved having Will around. Simon called him into his office. 'Have you thought about what you are going to do next? I spoke to Angie and she says Alf is covering everything brilliantly down there, just wondered if you would consider doing the same for us here?'

'Gosh, hadn't expected that to be honest. I'm not sure there is that much to do here, the place seems in pretty good shape now,' he replied, not wanting them to spend more money than was needed.

'I need someone who can sort out odd leaks and maintenance as they crop up and more importantly someone that fits in. How you are with the residents is just magical, I mean Margaret has opened up so much since you arrived. You could help us share practical ideas between the two homes as I don't have as much time as I'd like to pop down there. With some of our residents' more challenging behaviour, it is so important that I am here most of the time and of course, I know Primrose is in the very capable hands of Angie, which is a huge burden lifted.'

After a phone call to Alf and Angie, who both thought it was a brilliant idea, it was all agreed. He just needed to sort out somewhere to stay.

That evening, before he had chance to mention the new working arrangements at the care home, Sarah suddenly said that they needed to have a chat. She looked deadly serious and also quite sad but until Lily was in bed, she didn't want to talk about it. Clicking the baby monitor on in the lounge, she passed him a cup of tea and took a seat.

Unbeknown to Will she had been deliberating her life over the past couple of days. Having settled in quickly, she had finally had a bit of time to contemplate all that had happened and think about her. Brian had hurt her more than she had thought; really believing that deep down he loved her only to find out this was not and had probably never been the case. Her heart had been broken so many times in her life, and every time she grew attached to someone they left her or she was taken away. As a young girl she had really tried her best to fit in with her foster families, well the first few anyway. And every time she got settled and hoped that they would start loving her, even just a little bit, she had to leave and move somewhere else. They never wanted her to stay. She remembered vividly asking her social worker if she could be adopted, she hated having to move all the time. But apparently, people prefer babies and younger children, being seven years old and being a bit naughty sometimes, it was unlikely. And after the fourth move, she had learnt to build a hard barrier. Teenage years in the care home were just horrendous and best forgotten, strange men hanging around. She did her best to keep under the radar but it didn't always work. Alcohol definitely helped. She really believed Brian was the first person in her life to not use her and reject her again shortly afterwards, but how silly of her to expect any different. It was always just a matter of time. The self doubt had kicked in again already; Will deep down was probably no different.

Not letting Will into these thoughts she had been having, she said 'First, I want you to know that I couldn't have coped with everything and got through it without you. I will always be thankful to you for that and will always be your friend, but I have been thinking...'

Will's heart immediately sunk, he knew what was coming.

'While the divorce is yet to be finalised and now I am here, I think it would be better for both of us if we have a bit of space and see how things pan out. I would hate to hurt you, please know that, but need to check that like you said once 'that it's not a rebound thing.' We have gotten very close and know it could go further, but I think we should take a break. Let's see if this is how things are supposed to be. I will of course still see you at the home when we visit Margaret and maybe we could meet up at the park sometimes, but just for now think it would be best to leave it like that.'

Gulping back the sudden surge of emotion, he replied, 'If that's what you really want. I really hoped it could be different but respect you and if that's your decision, I guess that's that then,' and got up from the chair. Turning to put his cup of tea down, trying not to tear up, he grabbed his coat and quickly said goodbye. He hoped she would run after him, but as always in his life the door closed.

Getting in the car he was completely devastated. Driving off back to the B&B, he cried like he hadn't cried for years. *'What did you expect you Will? No-one ever stays!'* he said out loud, wondering if life would ever be any different. It always seemed ok for him to be kicked in the teeth and hurt, why? He wished he knew. Arriving at the B&B with red, puffy eyes he dove up to his room before anyone could see.

Sarah sat in her lounge and cried long into the night. When Lily started screaming the place down with her teething pain, she cuddled her crying silent tears. *'Maybe this was for the best'*, she kept trying to convince herself. If it was just the two of them, they couldn't get hurt so it would be worth it in the long run.

Simon noticed the difference in Will's demeanour the next day and asked if everything was ok, just got the usual 'fine thanks' and some poor excuse. Will worked longer days to finish quicker and by lunchtime on day four, they agreed he could leave and return the next week on their new arrangements. He made sure he wasn't there when Sarah and Lily visited Margaret, as everything was still too raw, so quickly left and drove home.

Alf and Max were delighted to find him in the kitchen when they got back from Primrose. Putting the kettle on, Alf instantly noticed that something was up.

'Talk to me,' he said, handing him a cup of tea.

'Nothing to say really. Everything is fine, anyway how are you guys?' he said, trying to change the subject.

'Blimmin hell Will, remember it's me. I'm not going to budge until you tell me,' he replied, smiling but looking really concerned.

So Will told him everything that had happened. Over an hour later, Alf still hadn't said a word, just listened the whole time in disbelief. Shaking his head, he said 'Like you Will, I know she's right for you and she knows it too really. Give her time, the dear lass has been hurt so much in her life hasn't she? With being put into care and then her husband doing this, not to mention being attacked. I would put money on her being really upset too, but just trying to protect herself from any more pain. You two are really so alike with what you have both been through too. You know yourself that's why you have never let anyone get close to you before, I mean we can't say you haven't had offers,' he said smiling at him, reassuringly. 'Don't avoid her - I know it's hard. But let her see that you will wait, patience is all it takes. Just wait for her to be in the right place, maybe the divorce being finalised will do it, who knows? Her life has been an awful whirlwind recently, she'll come around you'll see.'

If only he knew for sure that that was the case.

The three of them popped into Primrose the following morning. Everyone was delighted to see Will again, which made him smile and was a really good distraction from thinking too much.

Sarah was distraught that evening, having turned up to see Margaret to find that Will had finished and gone home. *'Stupid cow, just stop it. This is your choice,'* she said to herself, sat in the lounge beside herself again with tears. As much as she tried to convince herself that she had made the right decision, she missed him terribly, much more than she had expected but *'it will get easier in time,'* she told herself unconvincingly. Thinking more and more about him, he had never asked her for anything or expected anything, just seemed to like being with her for her. *'I mean god he has definitely seen me looking my worst and wasn't scared off!'* thinking back to the first time he arrived at the house. And that made her smile.

Half an hour away, Will was busying himself the best he could. It was great being back with Alf and Max but my god, he missed Sarah and Lily. They say absence makes the heart grow fonder, but he had no idea it would be this bad. He worried about them too as had loved being able to take care of them, like his own little family. Still, it was up to Sarah. He would always respect her wishes, but wished he knew whether he'd done something wrong.

A few days later, a letter arrived that he hadn't been expecting. Very rarely hearing from his parents, a birthday card and Christmas card if they remembered was about it for years now. So recognising the writing, he ripped the envelope quickly and began to read.

'Our darling William,

The Aussies still love us and our business however we have found ourselves needing some extra funds. So we've been racking our brains and decided that if we rented out the house back in England then that could provide a regular good source of income. I mean the place is really a bit big just for you, so contacted a local estate agent and were incredibly surprised to find out just how much we may be able to charge! A gentleman called Mr Burton from Burtons Property Ltd will be contacting you next week to take a look and begin finding some suitable tenants, so please ensure the house is in good order and nice and tidy.

We thought it would be good company for you too, see we do think of you darling!

Anyway, ta ta for now, won't keep you any longer as expect you may need to get busy cleaning!

Mummy and Daddy xx'

Slamming his hand down on the kitchen worktop, he couldn't believe it! 'What have I done?!' he shouted out loud, thinking with this and Sarah he must have done something pretty bad in a past life or something. An hour later, Alf arrived to find Will in a really bad mood. Seeing the letter on the side, Will just said 'help yourself, have a read,' and stomped off into the garden, with Max following close behind.

Reading it and making a brew, Alf arrived in the garden with a cuppa for them both. Sitting down next to him, he said 'I know life seems a bit shit at the moment, but it will work out. Your bloody awful parents have got a bloody cheek to ask you to get the place ready though, I wouldn't bother if I were you. I mean, we keep it nice anyway. Any thoughts on what you are going to do?'

'Not yet, but I'm not staying here living with complete bloody strangers that's for sure,' he replied, angrily.

Will had kept the house quite minimalistic and modern. Having sold or turfed out all of his parents' old fashioned furniture over the years, with some people surprised at how reasonably priced he had advertised it at, IKEA had proved a brilliant help and cost effective too. Deep down Will had always expected his parents to sell the house and use the money for their life in Oz; he was pleasantly surprised that they hadn't mentioned it. Apart from trips to the pub or chippy and car expenses, he had always lived quite frugally, making sure he put as much into his savings account each month as he could. He had always planned one day to move out and setup on his own, but the time had never appeared quite right, maybe until now.

Alf offered straight away that they could move into his old house, which was great for a temporary measure. He was young though and ought to look at getting his own place too.

But life had to carry on as normal for now, and there were two care homes that needed their attention. 'Oh by the way, would be it ok if I came up to Green Meadows with you today, give you a hand?' asked Alf the next morning.

'Sure, Angie not need you then?' replied Will.

'No, they have got the council coming in for an inspection so we made sure everything was ready last week, so got some time on my hands. I'm sure they would all like to see Max again too,' he said smiling, getting his bits together.

It was a lovely sunny drive up to Green Meadows, but longer than Will had hoped. Being based back at home now meant double the time to get there, but for now there was no choice. Maybe he would reconsider whether taking on the work there was such a great idea; he might suggest they try and find someone more local. He could help with finding and vetting them, if they wanted.

They walked in the front door to find dear Agnes sat at the bus stop. 'Did you pass the bus on your way?' she asked.

'Shouldn't be long Agnes,' replied Will, smiling at Jenny who was coming to take her into the lounge to join the others.

They had a busy morning sorting out some quite disgusting plumbing issues, finding some very odd things had tried to be flushed down the toilets. It did make them giggle though, 'Blimey we really do go full circle sometimes don't we, like little children,' said Alf, fishing a pair of socks and a plastic ball out.

With the toilets now sorted, they went to find Simon to see what else needed their attention. The residents were all just finishing their lunch and going out for a sit in the garden. With the place nearly empty, Will suddenly felt someone grab his hand.

'Brian, my love. Shall we dance?' Margaret said, grinning from ear to ear. 'Come on, I've missed this!' leading him into the dancing room. There were a few people sat in there having a rest, and this wouldn't do! 'I don't know what these people are doing in my lounge!' she exclaimed, 'Come on you three, off into the garden, I don't remember inviting you,' and she gently eased each of them out of their chairs and showed them to the door. As they shuffled away, she whisked him around. For someone with dementia, she was surprisingly agile.

Alf took a seat, smiling and watching Will carefully leading her around the floor. You could tell that this was when she was her happiest. Feeling a little tap on his shoulder, he turned to see Sarah smiling too. She crept in and took a seat, holding Lily who was fast asleep in her arms. And as Will turned and saw her, his heart skipped.

'Play it cool, she has told you how it is' he thought to himself but was so pleased to see her. As they came to a stop, he bowed and she curtsied as was always customary at the end of their dance. Alf quickly stood up, and said 'May I?' to Margaret and took her off onto the floor again.

Will took a seat, smiling at Lily. 'You two ok?' he asked.

'Yep, all good thanks. You?' she replied.

'Fine, keeping busy,' he replied and they both went quiet, watching the dance floor. Lily started stirring, ready for her bottle and Will was only too happy to have her transferred into his arms while Sarah went to warm her milk. Looking at her, cradled in his arms, he felt himself welling up. 'What I wouldn't give to be with you always,' he muttered, trying his hardest not to blink. And like she heard him, she took hold of his finger in her hand.

As she awoke, he passed her back to Sarah for her feed. Opening her eyes to see Will, Lily was having none of it, so Will fed her her bottle while Sarah went to chat to Simon about how Margaret was getting on. This of course was an excuse, as sitting so close to him it was difficult not to blurt out something stupid, *'that it was all a mistake and she had changed her mind, could they be together.'* Returning to find Lily had supped all of her bottle and was now happily sat on his lap, she had to keep playing it cool. Margaret came and sat next to Sarah, at which point Will said they had better be getting on with their work and he and Alf thanked Margaret for the dance and left them to it.

'Did you say anything?' Alf asked Will, once they left the room.

''Course not. It's on her terms isn't it; I find it so hard though. And seeing little Lily too,' and they went off to find out what else needed sorting.

The following week, they received the call from Mr Burton, arranging to view and to confirm the rentable value at 11.00am the next morning. As Will began showing him around, Max came to say hello.

'Oh, Mrs Charlick stated definitely no pets. Is that correct?' asked Mr Burton, looking slightly puzzled.

'Oh no, don't worry about that, pets will be fine. With the time difference, she has asked me to take over the arrangements for renting out the house, she just needs to know how much she can expect to receive,' and was blown away to hear how much the monthly rent would be.

'Are you sure, that seems so expensive?'

'It's a lovely large family home, and you have maintained it really well. Think someone will snap it up,' he said smiling and left the paperwork for Will to complete.

'Twelve hundred pounds per month and they don't even own it! Are they bloody mental?!' exclaimed Alf, on hearing how much.

A week later, with all the paperwork signed and Evelyn and Henry over the moon at hearing how much healthier their bank account was going to be soon, the first viewings were arranged. As Mr Burton had predicted, there was a huge amount of interest and Saturday morning they had four prospective visits lined up.

The first three families all seemed very nice and pleasant, and they were sure they would be perfect tenants but as they opened the door to the fourth person, they instantly knew if she liked it she would be the one to move in! Glancing at each other with a smile, as the little Chihuahua barked angrily at them from inside her handbag, they were introduced to Ms Salmon. With a kind face, her dress sense was quite eccentric and the first thing she wanted to look at was the garden, *'for all her little darlings.'*

In a very posh voice, which Evelyn would definitely approve of, she was delighted to see the large lawned garden was completely enclosed. 'I couldn't bear it if one of them escaped, this is perfect,' she said.

'Oh one of them, so you have more than your little dog then?' asked Will, smiling at the dog growling at him.

'Oh my goodness yes. This is Tinkerbell; she can't bear to be away from me. I have seven dogs and three cats and the agent said you were ok with pets - that is ok isn't it? I think your house would be perfect for us,' replied Ms Salmon smiling.

'Oh yes, the more the merrier, we love animals!' said Will, delighted that Ms Salmon liked the place, knowing his mum and dad would go completely ballistic if they were here now.

All the paperwork was agreed and signed, and with Evelyn and Henry only interested in the monetary side, a moving-in date arranged. Having had most of the IKEA furniture for many years, Will decided to give it away rather than put it in storage. There wasn't enough room at Alf's to store it and storage was so expensive – not worth it at all. A new place one day and a new start (with new furniture) Will decided would be the best option. The local charity for helping poor families were delighted with the offer, arriving with a van the next day to collect all the items Will was happy to pass on.

Meanwhile, Alf had been busily getting the spare room ready for Will's arrival. He hadn't had anyone live in his house since dear Elsie, and was kind of looking forward to it. Having spent most of the time at Will's for a long time now, he flew down to the shops to get some supplies.

Ms Salmon arrived promptly at 10.00am to begin the mammoth task of settling in all her pets and their accessories. Each had their own bed, water and feeding bowls and enough food to feed an animal shelter for probably about a year. Breezing through the door, she looked so happy. They made sure the lounge doors were kept shut, so no animal could escape, and Alf and Will gave her a hand. 'You are really very kind to help me, thank you,' she said, smiling as she squeezed pass them in the hall with yet more animal food. Once all the animals were in and safe, she said she would be fine as was now just waiting for her removal van to arrive with all her furniture. Giving them both a firm handshake, they said their goodbyes with Max watching everything from the backseat of the car.

'Oh my god, can you imagine my parents if they could see our house now!' said Will, bursting out laughing and muttered a quick goodbye to the house, wondering where he would end up eventually.

Arriving at Alf's, Will was so touched that Alf had made such an effort. He had his own chair in the lounge, opposite Alf and Elsie's, and his bedroom was made up ready for him, with everything smelling beautifully clean. A casserole was in the oven and as he was passed a beer, he suddenly felt really content. Whilst the Sarah situation was still very sad, he had to appreciate what he did have which was the best friend you could possibly hope for. All the things they had been through together, whoever would have imagined or predicted how their life from teacher and pupil would change.

Life settled into a routine. Taking care of both care homes was really busy and they had lots of fun with the residents too. Both sites were completely full with waiting lists for each and you could see why. Will bumped into Sarah and Lily regularly, which was getting less awkward each time and just tried to take it in his stride. If Alf was right, which he usually was, she was worth waiting for so he just needed to be patient. It did sadden him a bit that she seemed to have moved on so quickly and was obviously not missing him at all. He had no idea that Sarah was feeling exactly the same, which reinforced her belief that he would have moved on and left her in the end anyway, as already he doesn't seem that bothered and quite happy with life. Lily was growing fast and was totting about the place, much to the amusement of everyone. With Margaret still finding him for her regular dance, he loved the short time he had with them all together.

The phone ringing at 3.30am was completely unexpected.

'Will, so sorry to wake you but couldn't get hold of Brian,' Simon said anxiously. 'I've left an urgent message for him but it's Margaret. She has collapsed and been rushed into hospital, Sarah is on her way, with Lily of course as there is no-one that could look after her and I didn't know who else to call.'

'Thanks for letting me know, I'll get there as soon as I can. I can at least help with Lily, if nothing else,' replied Will, frantically pulling on some trousers while hanging up. Quietly tapping on Alf's door, he went in to see Alf was awake – he had heard the phone too. 'Go now, I'll sort everything here and at the homes, you need to be there,' he whispered, smiling at him.

At 4.30am he arrived at St Matthew's Hospital. Rushing up to the desk, he was asked to take a seat as he wasn't family. Half an hour later, Sarah appeared with Lily, tear streaks all down her face. She was so pleased to see him and thankful that Simon had thought to phone him. Brian still hadn't arrived; she had left him over ten messages as it wasn't looking good. Lily was asleep in her car seat, oblivious to her mum's distress. 'What am I going to do Will? She can't die!' she sobbed.

Trying Brian's number yet again, and still no answer, she asked Will to come and sit with her. 'Margaret would like that you are here,' she said, giving him a little smile. Entering the room, he suddenly felt an overwhelming sadness. Margaret was completely still, with some machines bleeping, her eyes closed. 'Has she spoken yet?' asked Will.

Sarah shook her head.

They each took a seat either side of her and sat in silence, holding her hand. 'They say they might still be able to hear, don't they?' and she started quietly talking to her about how Lily was getting on with walking now and what they had been up to.

'If you can hear me, please squeeze my hand, just so I know you are ok,' she said, tears streaming again.

Nothing.

A short time later she motioned for Will to come out of the room with her. In the corridor outside, she said 'Are you alright to look after Lily for a minute, while I try and get hold of Brian again?'

''Course,' replied Will and took hold of the car seat, with Lily still sound asleep.

Appearing again, she looked upset and really mad. 'He can't come - he's on his way from the hotel to the airport.

Think I heard someone with him too, not that that matters anymore. But even with a chance that his mum might pass away, he still isn't coming, can you believe it?! He just said, *'with the dementia she won't even know if I am there or not anyway.'*

'Lucky she has you,' said Will, shaking his head.

They were asked to go out while the doctor and nurse did some more observations and tests. Grabbing a quick coffee from the vending machine, they waited in silence outside ready to be allowed back in. As the door opened, the doctor asked to speak to Sarah in a room nearby. As Will heard her cry from in the corridor, he knew the news wasn't good. Margaret was dying and probably only had a few hours, 'We are very sorry but she is comfortable and not in pain,' the doctor explained.

Sobbing uncontrollably, she took a seat next to Will in the corridor, updating him on the news she had been praying she wouldn't hear. He put his arm around her and let her cry into his chest, a cry that was so deep it hurt. 'She can't leave me as well,' she whispered, sobbing.

Trying to stop the tears the best she could, they went back to be with Margaret. Each holding her hand, Sarah quietly comforted her, saying 'if she had to go and be with Ron again, that is ok, she would understand. But she wanted her to know that she had loved her more than anyone else in her life and thanked her for everything.' Tears now fell down Will's cheeks too.

At 6.42am they both felt a sudden slight squeeze of their hands, two tears fell down Margaret's cheeks and she took her last breath. It was so incredibly sad, but for Margaret it was very peaceful - she just went to sleep. Crying her heart out, Sarah sobbed 'please god, let this just be a bad dream and let me wake up. I don't know think I can cope with this anymore, always being left on my own.' It was too sad to stay any longer, so she gave Margaret a final kiss and hug goodbye and left the room.

Out in the corridor Will placed Lily, still fast asleep in her car seat, on the floor and put his arms out to Sarah. She sobbed into his chest, with her arms tight around his waist. They stayed like that for a few minutes until Sarah looked up at him. 'Thank you for being here,' she said.

'I just want you to know I would never hurt or leave you Sarah, I love you,' he said, tears streaming down his face now. She took his face in her hands and kissed him.

He insisted on following her home in the car, to make sure she was ok. Driving behind her, he cried most of the way too: he was sad for Margaret, sad for Sarah but it also brought back all the emotion of losing Mabel. He suddenly felt twelve years old again, with that deep ache in his chest of sadness and loss.

Arriving back at the cottage, she invited him in, so he quickly phoned Alf to give him the very sad news. Lily began stirring, ready for her breakfast. Sarah couldn't believe that she had actually slept through the night, not something she had ever done before, maybe she knew too.

On seeing Will, Lily's arms flew up for him to pick her up. Wrapping her little arms around his neck, she nuzzled into his shoulder, holding on so tight like she was never going to let go. Sarah looked completely shattered, so he suggested she go and have a couple of hours sleep, while he gave Lily her breakfast and looked after her.

Fully clothed, Sarah collapsed onto the bed and pulled the duvet over her. She just cried and cried into her pillow until she fell asleep. Waking to see the alarm clock saying 1.00pm, she ripped back the duvet and ran down the stairs. She found Lily in absolute stitches of laughter, with Will chasing her around the garden. The picnic blanket was on the lawn, covered in toys and yoghurt and as Will turned around to see her watching them, she laughed as she saw the splats of yoghurt that had somehow ended up in his hair. *'See, he is different to all the others you stupid girl, and he even said he loved you,'* she said to herself, taking them out a cup of tea.

After tea, and checking she was going to be ok, he reminded her that he was just at the end of the phone, and left to go back to Alf's. She hadn't said a word about what he had blurted out at the hospital, caught up in all the emotion he hadn't planned for it to come out like that. Will was kicking himself – he hoped she wouldn't think he was trying to take advantage of her when she was at her most vulnerable.

Two weeks later, it was the day of the funeral. Although they had spoken on the phone, they hadn't seen each other as there was no need for her to visit the home now. The heavens opened, with the rain lashing down as everyone huddled around the grave. Brian had arrived late and missed most of the church service, but at least he was there now. Will had offered to take care of Lily if she started playing up, which of course she did almost immediately. Watching from afar, with Lily running around with her hood tightly done up, they found a small patch of forget-me-nots, Margaret's favourite flower, and picked a small bunch. As the coffin was lowered into the ground, Sarah stood motionless, gulping back the sobs, tears flowing steadily down her cheeks. Will carried Lily over to join them, holding her little bunch of flowers, and held her tightly while she dropped them. As they landed gently on top of the coffin, they each blew Margaret a kiss and he carried her off again. Brian said very little and was in a hurry afterwards to get back to his car. He wouldn't be able to attend the wake as he, '*didn't really know anyone there anyway,*' and Sarah watched him leave with a female in the front passenger seat.

Simon, and as many of the staff from the home that they could afford to let have the time off, were there and they all raised a toast to '*our Margaret.*' Playing her favourite song, they all joined each other on the dance floor in her memory, Will dancing with Sarah holding Lily. 'She would love this,' she said, starting to cry again. It was such an emotional day but also time to share some really lovely and funny stories. Everyone was in hysterics hearing about the stepping stone nappies! Helping clear up afterwards, Sarah couldn't stop thanking Simon for everything and giving Margaret the great end to her life that she couldn't do for her on her own. He made her promise to keep in touch as she'd grown so close to all of them; she'd become a part of their family.

Dropping her back home afterwards, Lily insisted that it wasn't Will's home time yet. Finally putting her to bed at 8.30pm, she was out like a light. Coming back down the stairs, he found Sarah with a glass of wine. She looked completely drained and empty. 'You ok? I mean I know it's a stupid thing to say, of course you're not. But will you be ok here?' he asked.

'I'll have to be, won't I. Can I ask you something? Would you mind staying just for tonight, don't feel like being on my own?'

'Of course, I'll sleep down here.'

She got him a beer while he phoned Alf to let him know he would be back tomorrow, but not to get excited, '*it's just for tonight because of the funeral today*'. They sat and chatted long into the night, and ended up falling asleep with her tucked under his arm on the sofa. Waking up to Lily chatting away on the baby monitor in her own funny little language, they both smiled at each other.

'I'm really sorry for pushing you away. I just get so scared that everyone always leaves me or decides they prefer someone else, and I get so hurt. If it wasn't for Lily and Margaret, I'm not sure I'd still be here you know. And you of course. I think I have fallen in love with you, but I'm so scared to admit it because I can't risk anything for Lily. It's not just me I have to think about,' she said looking up at him, eyes going all glassy.

'Sarah you know my past. Why do you think I have always been on my own, because like you, everyone always leaves me. I promise knowing how that feels, I will never go, I love you.'

Staring into his eyes and smiling, she got up and kissed him, whispering 'I love you too,' as she went to get Lily, who had now started yelling for her breakfast. Sarah and Will then spent the morning chatting about how things could work. They would take it slowly for now, with him staying over occasionally but them living in their separate homes.

'See blimmin told you so!' exclaimed Alf excitedly, as Will arrived home to tell him the news.

After having a quick catch up, they both went to Primrose together as Angie had phoned with some new ideas she wanted to discuss with them. Whilst most of the residents just needed care, she had noticed some deterioration in their memory and them getting concerned about it. The day before, wandering around the corridor, Alan had got himself in a pickle as he couldn't remember which was his room and had walked in on Betty getting undressed, who screamed and shouted at him.

Running to his aid, she had reassured both of them that it was 'easily done and nothing to worry about, come on as the Beetle Drive is about to start!' and with that, they had both moved on quickly.

As they pulled up in the car, Angie was just taking in the post and waved. Max was first out of the car and trundled off into the home, while she began telling them about the recent events and how she thought putting their photos on their bedroom door would be a helpful check for them. 'If everyone does it, it won't single out anyone who maybe needs more help.'

Will remembered seeing a laminating machine at Green Meadows, so said he would ask Simon if they could borrow it, bringing it back with him in the next couple of days (all being well). It would be a good excuse for him to make a visit somewhere else too.

Wondering where Max had gone, he went to find out. There he was in Sylvie's room, getting lots of fuss. 'Oh he's fine, I love it to be truthful. He always comes to find me,' she said smiling. Alf suddenly appeared too and Will couldn't help but notice the way they were talking and looking at each other. Maybe he wasn't the only one who had found someone special.

As they left to go back home, Sylvie came out to wave them off and say goodbye to Max. Getting into the car, smiling at Alf, Will asked 'Anything I need to know?'

'Don't be bloody daft,' he replied, with a little smirk. 'But she has become a really good friend. You know, we have such a similar past and it's been lovely getting to know her more and more. She is always the first to offer me a cuppa, even though she is a resident and it isn't her place to. She recently bought a little kettle for her room - Angie says it's so she can make me a cup of tea. It's their little secret as she wouldn't want any of the other residents having one in their room - too dangerous. But Sylvie is only there for company and to ease the loneliness, she doesn't really need caring for.'

'Have you ever thought about taking her out for lunch or something?' Will asked.

'Not really. Like you, we have just gradually become good friends. You've got me thinking though, I wonder if she would like that? I mean it's a home not a prison, maybe I should pluck up the courage and ask her?'

'I think she would love that,' Will replied.

The following day, Will made his way to Green Meadows while Alf set off for Primrose.

While Alf was greeted with a cup of tea and then began cracking on with all the little jobs that had been lined up for him, Will was struggling. Maybe it was grief, he didn't know, but whilst everyone was their lovely selves he felt an overwhelming feeling of sadness. Half expecting his dance partner to come around the door to see if he had time for just a quick dance, he hadn't imagined how much he would miss her.

Simon turned up with a cup of tea, and they sat and chatted about Angie's ideas. 'I've got some templates too for a 'make-yourself' photo family tree if that would be of any use?' Simon offered.

'Sounds great, I'll pass them onto Angie for you,' Will replied.

'You ok?' asked Simon, noticing he wasn't his jovial self.

'Yes thanks, just struggling a bit today, never realised how much I would miss her,' he replied.

'We have all had tears about Margaret, and at least one of us still does every day. It is so hard, but she was really happy here and that's what we have to remember,' Simon said, patting him on the shoulder.

'Yes I know. Sarah really misses coming up here too, think she feels a bit lost sometimes,' said Will.

'I heard that the two of you had gotten quite close, we are all so chuffed as she is such a lovely girl. Do tell her from us that she is welcome here anytime, Lily too,' Simon replied smiling.

'Thanks, she'll appreciate that. I think it might be hard just now, with it being so soon after Margaret passing, but I know she would definitely like to come and say hello to everyone soon,' said Will.

Finishing his tea, he said he had better start cracking on with the jobs list and thanked him for the laminator. Simon turned up a short time later to show him the template he was talking about, *'it really helps knowing a bit about their family and gives a nice talking point in their rooms. Great little prompt for when the memory is struggling with who is who, means a lot to them and gives us something nice to talk about and reminisce with them,'* he explained.

Piling everything into the car, he said his goodbyes saying he would see them in two days, and set off to see Sarah and Lily. They had a really lovely evening, with Will giving Sarah a break by happily giving Lily her bath and bedtime story. Going back down the stairs, he was greeted with a huge smile and a beer – perfect! They chatted about anything and everything, it was so easy and both ended up in tears about Margaret. Collapsing into bed at 1.30am, both exhausted from their days, they instantly fell asleep in each other arms.

But at 5.30am they were woken abruptly with Lily screaming the house down, and went in to find she was unfortunately a bit poorly. Rosy red cheeks, with an obvious temperature, and her other end absolutely honking and something vile dripping out of her nappy, Sarah picked her up out of her cot at arm's length. With Will laughing holding onto his nose, she said 'Here you are, welcome to parenthood!' as Lily grabbed hold of him, her nappy contents spilling out onto his top.

'Blimmin hell Missy, let's get you hosed down and cleaned up,' and raced her through to the bathroom. Hosing her down, he patted her dry and put on a fresh nappy and pyjamas and quickly grabbed himself a new top too. Feeling very sorry for herself, she just clung onto him. They both appeared downstairs to find Sarah making them both a drink in the kitchen. She wrapped her arms around both of them, smiling.

Waving them off a short while later, he said he would phone later to see how they were both doing. Sarah wandered back into the house, smiling as for the first time in such a long time she had support, someone had her back.

Will had arranged to drive straight to Primrose and meet Alf there. Reception was very quiet and walking through the lounge, they heard lots of giggling and singing. Entering the activity room, they found all the residents with the children, having a great time having their photos taken. Angie was then handing them the Polaroid to stick onto the paper, with the children helping find the letters for their names and then sticking them above the photos. Lots of glitter and stickers were added to decorate their poster, with lots of it seeming to land on the floor and in their hair too! Will set up the laminator and they each took turns to get their poster sealed. The children then each went with their person to help put it on the door and have a quick nosey in their rooms. Alf, Will and the team of carers were all on hand to help, and by lunchtime each bedroom door was clearly labelled.

Thanking all the children for their help, they said their goodbyes and went to collapse in their chairs before lunch was called. It had been a fun morning and Angie was thrilled with the results. 'No getting mixed up now,' she said, beaming at Will and Alf. The residents really seemed to appreciate it too, always making them smile as they got back to their room, seeing what they and the children had produced.

Once Angie had everyone seated for lunch, Will showed her the templates Simon had passed on. She thought it was a fabulous idea. Will said he and Alf could make something to frame them to put them up on their bedroom walls. It ended up being a great talking point, with everyone sat at the table sorting out who was who, labelling them and putting them in the space they wanted. It didn't matter that they were in the correct order; more important was who they were and their relation to them.

Whenever anyone came to live at the home, Angie had always tried to make sure to ask their family for any spare photos with information written on the back, that she would keep and be able to talk to them about. Whilst the residents had brought their own photos, they couldn't believe it when Angie arrived with some old photos they hadn't seen for years - even she had forgotten about some of them too. Seeing people they hadn't seen for years, it brought back many happy memories and some really funny comments as well. They obviously hadn't missed some of them, and the ones that they were rude about were put back in their file rather than added to the template. Lots of giggles and a few swear words were had; it turned out to be a really fun activity that everyone enjoyed immensely.

'I must say, you're looking really well Will. We did really miss you but looks like working at Green Meadows has done you the power of good,' Angie said to him a day or so later.

'Thanks, yes feel quite happy thanks.'

'Anyone we might know or did you meet someone there?' she asked smiling.

'Bloody hell, has Alf been talking! Actually I did meet someone there, we are taking things slowly though, see how it goes. Can you really tell?' he answered smiling back.

'Yes I can and am just so chuffed for you Will, you so deserve it,' she replied.

When they were leaving Will nudged Alf, 'well, did you ask her then?' he said.

'No, just didn't feel like the right time and also need to decide where to take her first,' Alf replied.

'What are the options?'

'Could go to the pub or the cafe at the garden centre, she loves gardening,' Alf answered.

'Well either sounds great, why don't you take her for lunch and a mooch about the garden centre. It's really casual and our local one does fab lunches. Have you ok'd it with Angie?' he asked.

'Nope, not plucked up courage for that either.'

'Well now's as good a time as any, go on,' and pushed him back towards the door, just as Angie was coming out the front.

Asking if he was alright, he finally asked if it would be ok to take Sylvie out for lunch, if of course she said she would like to. 'I'm sure she will love that, yes of course,' said Angie, and took him by the arm to go and find Sylvie.

Sylvie was over the moon at being asked and they arranged it for two days time. The two days flew past and Alf arrived ten minutes early to find Sylvie waiting for him at the front door. 'Thank you so much,' she said, looking so happy.

They had a lovely time together, wandering around all the plants, discussing their favourites and the nightmare ones that always seemed to die and then enjoyed a delicious lunch in the cafe. Taking her back to the home a few hours later, she thanked him and hoped maybe they could do it again sometime. He agreed he would love that, especially if she would like to think of where they would like to go next time. He got in the door with a new spring in his step, a companion that would never be able to take Elsie's place but could fill a little part of the gaping hole she left behind. *'You would like her too,'* he said quietly, patting her chair in the lounge.

Will could tell it had gone well and sitting with a beer each in the evening, with the football on the TV, they both looked happier than they had in a long time.

* * *

Lives elsewhere were not going so well.

Sharon and Claire had served half of their sentences and were both released with a strict curfew between 8.00pm and 7.00am every day.

Claire's in-laws had disowned her and with that considerable strain on their relationship, inevitably her marriage broke down too. So she was now living back at home with her mum who, with advanced dementia, was driving her to a near nervous breakdown. She couldn't get away either, this was her curfew address.

Sharon had promised Liam she would wait for him, visiting him as often as she could. She had been granted supervised contact with the children, which Gary and the children were dreading but he was trying to keep a brave face and kept telling them how 'mum was really missing them and would be so excited to spend some time with them at last.' They had all settled so well, it was like a new life for them all, a very happy life too. He should have realised though that he had little to worry about. Not showing up at the first meeting and not answering her phone, she had been told in no uncertain terms that this was unacceptable. She was given another chance but arrived three hours late *'pissed as a fart,'* stinking of beer - luckily the children had long gone home. She was told she would receive a court summons shortly regarding the permanent full custody being awarded to Gary, with no access being granted. She hated the hostel she was living in, having lost her house. And with Liam having his sentence regularly extended, due to the incidents of drugs and fighting inside, her life wasn't going to be changing any time soon either.

*

Brian continued sleeping around; however he apparently had picked on the wrong one last time, again dumping her as usual by text. Natalie wasn't to be messed with and had secretly filmed him snorting cocaine only a few hours before needing to be up for a return flight. This was sent for the attention of his boss who fired him on the spot. There was no denying the evidence and they couldn't risk this coming out in the open, a PR disaster for the airline.

Things then got even worse for Brian. Having slept with most of the girls in the village, and with no income coming in, he'd had no choice but to put the house on the market. The agents had confirmed that he couldn't have picked a worse time to try and sell, and was likely to lose at least £100,000 on the purchase price. And with no job, pilot's uniform and a much reduced bank balance, suddenly found himself to be less attractive than he thought to the opposite sex so had turned to drink even more.

Following the funeral, he had only contacted Sarah once, which was to ask whether there was any refund due from the home for her fees that she may have paid in advance. *'Oh my god, you are such an idiot! Ask them your bloody self!'* was her answer as she hung up. She received monthly payments for Lily for a short time but as his circumstances changed, she received a solicitor's letter informing her that they would shortly be stopping. He wasn't interested in seeing Lily either and they had included a note from him, regarding adoption. He apparently had heard she was with someone new now, and if she felt it was right, he would happily sign adoption papers for Lily to have a new dad. She asked for them to be put on file for now.

*

With the recession being worldwide, the business world in Oz had also taken a nosedive. While the rent had helped initially with some of their bills, it was now only covering the interest on their loans. They had frantically been trying to get hold of William to see if he could sell some of the furniture and get the bank to wire them the money, as some of their creditors were getting a bit shitty! But with no reply, they guessed he must be out all the time. Reluctantly they had decided they had no choice but to return to the UK, and arriving back at Heathrow were getting very frustrated at William's lack of response to their letters and messages.

They pulled up outside the house with the most horrendous jetlag. 'Just need to get in, have a big sleep and then bloody well find out what our son thinks he is playing at, not getting back to us!' announced Evelyn.

Having treated Ms Salmon, their tenant, horrendously and insisting on immediate vacation of their home, she'd had no choice but to just up and leave. There had been no time to do any cleaning. As Evelyn opened the door, the honk of dog and cats made her immediately gag and gasp for air. 'Henry, Henry! I can't breathe! That god awful smell!' and she began to retch, just before she fainted and hit the floor. You could have heard the thud six miles away. Phoning the agent, threatening to sue, he popped over with all the signed paperwork, highlighting the 'pets allowed' part.

Deleting all the messages he got, Will decided he had to put a stop to this once and for all. They had never really wanted him in their lives, so he wrote his final letter informing them that he had moved on long ago and if he continued to receive the calls and messages, would report them for harassment. It was just a matter of convenience that they were suddenly now in touch, and tough shit on them this time. He had a good life now and they were definitely not ever going to be part of it, '*I have a new family now and am truly happy, no thanks to you two. Ta ta, (as you would say) Will xx.* He felt such a sense of satisfaction as he licked the stamp and posted the letter. He heard later that they ended up having to sell the house to pay off their debts and had moved into a local mobile home park, which made him smile too. 'Don't think they will be inviting their snooty friends around any time soon, poor people at the park, I feel sorry for them,' he said, updating Sarah on what he'd heard.

*

Robbie and his dad were not having a good time at all inside their separate prisons. With one being a head of the police, corrupt at that, and the other a rapist and the son of a policeman, this hadn't gone down well with the other prisoners one bit. Occasionally they seemed to be left alone, with no prison officers around to protect them, and got a bit of comeuppance. No-one could ever help with what had happened and the CCTV always seemed to have had an error just at that moment in time, weird!

The grandparents, who were both lovely and completely shocked and devastated at what had come to light, were found a lovely retirement home by the sea, for them to see out their last years. It was more expensive than Mr Gibbons had planned, but as it was taken out of his hands and paid from the proceeds of selling the house, he had had no part in that decision. Having found a huge stash of seized drugs at the house, all of the leftover proceeds were split between drug rehabilitation schemes and victim support of sexual violence. Selling both the properties in the UK and Spain, both charities had benefitted enormously. If they survived life inside, on release they would both be housed in hostel accommodation. They were both getting exactly what they deserved.

* * *

On the other hand, many lives had taken an upward turn.

Simon and Angie were a terrific team, running both homes with such love and care. This hadn't gone unnoticed, with the local press getting wind of the awards they had both received and publicising them regularly, they now had waiting lists as long as your arm. This in turn also meant that there was no way Simon was going to risk Angie being headhunted, so he gave her a large increase in salary. And with her husband Andy now working part time around the girl's school hours, they booked their first ever family holiday. She couldn't believe the change in her life and how happy they could be.

Sarah and Will spent more and more time together, and both finally agreed that things were so good that it would be crazy not to live together. They just needed to find the right place and also speak to Alf. This would be the hardest part. Sarah and Alf had also become very close, like a second dad to her and grandad to Lily too. He absolutely adored Lily.

They looked around the villages local to Sarah, as it was half way between each care home, deciding that this would be the best area for everyone. Will had just got off the phone from the local estate agent. 'He has just been to visit and price a house that he thinks would be perfect for us. The owner has agreed to put it on the market through them and he thinks it may be just what we are looking for,' he told Sarah excitedly.

'Let's arrange to see it then?' she replied grinning, and he immediately phoned them back, arranging to view the next afternoon at 4.00pm.

It was perfect. Similar to the cottage she was renting but slightly bigger, it just gave you that feeling the minute you stepped through the door. There was also a two bedroom cottage in the grounds; they couldn't believe they could possibly afford it. 'The lady that owns it is finding it too much now, way too big for her now her husband has passed and her children left home. She needs someone that can move quickly, without a large chain, as is looking into going into care herself. She's getting a little bit forgetful but more than anything, she wants company and someone else to do the cooking and cleaning. To enjoy her final years,' he explained.

And they both immediately looked at each other, with what they thought could be the perfect solution. Telling him they might be able to help the lady with that too, if she could just wait for a few days, they would come back to view again and hopefully have a very exciting proposition. With the housing market being quiet, and particularly in small villages like this, he said he was sure she would be fine with that and looked forward to hearing back from them. He also promised not to show anyone else around before he had spoken to them first.

Bursting with excitement, they jumped back in the car, and looking at each other they knew exactly what the other was thinking. They got to Alf's house to find him happily on the phone to Sylvie.

'Yes, yes of course, I would love that too. Think I know just the place,' he said, smiling at them both as they came through the door. 'Yes love, see you at 11.00am tomorrow then,' and hung up.

'Blimey what's up with you two? Won the lottery?' he said, seeing the excitement in their faces. Lily had been so good all day but was now deciding to let rip, so they popped her out in the garden with Max. They sat with a cup of tea at the table with Alf and told him all about the house viewing. Seeing him trying his best to look really happy, but could sense the same sadness they had felt about the prospect of leaving him, told him all about the two bedroom cottage. His face melted, and a few tears trickled down his cheeks. 'Do you really mean it?' he asked quietly.

'Wouldn't want it any other way, please say yes!' they both squealed.

He got up, thanked them and hugged them both, feeling so incredibly emotional. He had always vowed never to leave his and Elsie's home but knew at the same time she wouldn't want him to stay and be lonely and unhappy. He would have wanted the same for her. But at the same time he never imagined a time when he would get a new chance to be happy somewhere else. They insisted of course, that he must come and see it again with them on the second viewing, to see what he thought.

'That's all lovely, but before that I have just arranged with Sylvie to take her out for fish and chips tomorrow, picking her up at 11.00am. And you know Will, I was thinking of taking her to the sea, what do you think?'

'I think that would be lovely,' Will replied smiling, 'Elsie would too.'

'Oh blimey, you have got to stop doing this to me,' he said, as the tears began flowing again. 'Think working in these care homes has done me no good at all, soppy old git,' he said smiling, dabbing his eyes with his hankie. 'Do you guys fancy coming?'

'If you're sure - we'd love that!' said Sarah, before Will could answer, 'Lily has never been to the beach.'

'That's that then - let's take both cars down, you follow me ok?'

'Fab,' they replied and left to go and find Lily, who was being worryingly quiet. Finding her in the garden, hands in the soil and with mud all over her top, she waddled up to Sarah feeling very pleased with herself as she had found a worm that she thought mummy might like to eat!

They all set off the next morning, really looking forward to their day out. And no-one more than Sylvie. She had really grown very fond of Alf and looked forward to his visits so much. She just hoped that whilst he wasn't a spring chicken himself, he would be able to continue working at the care home so they got to see each other over half of the week. Alf felt exactly the same, but had just never said.

The sun was shining and the sea glistening, with a slight breeze it was the perfect day to be by the sea. Will and Sarah went off with Lily to get the food and drinks, whilst Alf and Sylvie took a seat on the bench. Max was getting on a bit now but still loved to chase the ball with his new friend Monty, Sarah's dog. And as they sat eating their food, it was the picture of contentment. After lunch they all went for a walk on the beach, and let Lily have a paddle in the sea which she absolutely loved. Giggling as the water splashed her face, and with Max and Monty running in and out of the waves, their afternoon was filled with sandcastles, ice cream and running after the ball. Like one big happy family.

Dropping Sylvie back to the home later, she couldn't stop thanking him for such a lovely day. He had also told her about Will and Sarah's idea for a possible house move, which he noticed made Sylvie suddenly go very quiet. 'You ok Sylvie, something I said?' he asked, a bit concerned he had upset her.

'Oh yes, absolutely fine thank you Alf. Just worry that if you move away, that maybe you won't be able to visit so much. Oh gosh, can't believe I said that out loud, silly me,' she said, blushing slightly.

'If it was blimmin Aberdeen I would still come and visit, don't think you can get rid of me that easily young lady,' he said, grinning at her.

'I'd really miss you, you know.'

'And I would miss you too,' he said, also slightly blushing now. 'Good god, what are we like?!'

'Never thought after Tom I would find such a good friend and companion,' she said taking hold of his hand and kissing him on the cheek.

'Crikey, the fish and chips must have been good!' he joked. 'No being serious, I would love it if you would come and have a look with us too, would you like that? I'd really appreciate your thoughts.'

'Would love to,' she replied.

'Right then, once I know when, I will call and arrange to come and pick you up,' he replied smiling. He got out of the car and opened her door, giving her a quick hug and kiss on the cheek, before she walked back up to the home. Angie opened the door and waved, putting her arm around Sylvie to take her back in.

The following Saturday at 11.00am, Will, Sarah, Lily, Alf and Sylvie all arrived for the viewing and as they turned into the small gravel drive at the front of the house, Alf and Sarah separately suddenly felt choked. As you turned in off the road, on either side were flowerbeds filled with forget-me-nots and hyacinths; Margaret and Elsie's favourite flowers. What a welcome!

As they walked up to the entrance, the estate agent was stood smiling waiting for them. Ethel, the lady who owned the house, also wanted to meet them so came out to say hello. As they walked around, admiring the beautiful rooms and garden, she just watched. Having spent over an hour exploring both cottages and the garden, and the most perfect workshop, they met back at the front with the estate agent waiting with bated breath for their answer.

'We absolutely love it!' said Sarah and Will holding hands. 'What do you think Alf?' they said, turning to him.

'I agree, it's absolutely lovely. It would be a pleasure and honour to live somewhere like here, I mean this is fairytale stuff for goodness sake, but don't think I could possibly afford it.'

'What if you had some help with that?' came a voice. 'If you would have me, I would love to come and be here with you all too?!' said Sylvie.

'You sure my love? I'm sure I can be a crotchety old git sometimes,' he said smiling at her.

'Remember I lived with you at the home for all those weeks, think we got on pretty well too,' she said smiling back.

'Do you need to give much notice on your room?' asked the estate agent, 'Ethel would like to move as quickly as possible.'

'Well yes I do, but my home going to the right people is just as important to me,' said Ethel, suddenly joining in the conversation. 'May I ask where you live now?'

'Primrose care home, about thirty minutes from here. It's absolutely lovely,' replied Sylvie.

'Well, maybe I should come and have a look there. Does it stink of wee?' she asked, quite seriously.

'Oh no, it's so lovely,' chuckled Sylvie.

'No time like the present, can I go and have a look now?' asked Ethel.

'No problem at all. I can take you as need to drop Sylvie back anyway, it would be a pleasure,' offered Alf, and with that Ethel grabbed her handbag, locked the door and got in the car.

They chatted incessantly all the way there, answering her many questions and she couldn't believe it when the front door opened and they were all greeted so warmly by Angie. Sylvie quickly explained everything that had happened to Angie and she of course, was only too happy to show Ethel around and introduce her to everyone. She had arrived just in time to join in their afternoon tea, dance and haircut session which she joined in with straight away.

Thanking everyone for their time, she felt a bit teary leaving as had had such little company for so long. 'I can't really believe how things have turned out, I was absolutely dreading selling the place but couldn't cope there any more on my own, thank you,' she said.

'We can't wait for you to come and live with us,' replied Angie, giving her a big hug.

Twelve weeks later, with all the legalities finalised, contracts exchanged and completed, it was moving day. The estate agent couldn't quite believe how easy this one had gone, with such little work on his part. Everyone had been in contact with each other and become good friends. Will and Alf were both feeling completely shattered packing up Sylvie, Ethel, Alf's house and Sarah's cottage - a mammoth task in such a short time, while of course still working. But it had all been worth it.

Will was in charge of moving Sarah and Lily first with the van. Alf collected Ethel and her personal affects, taking her to Primrose ready to collect Sylvie. Angie and Sylvie had completely blitzed her room and filled it with fresh flowers ready for Ethel's arrival. Angie was fine as she got busy helping Ethel with her stuff and showing her to her room, but saying goodbye to Sylvie got quite emotional.

'I'll miss you all, but will come back with Alf to visit if that's ok?' said Sylvie.

'Oh yes, please do. It has been an absolute pleasure having you living with us Sylvie, you will be greatly missed,' and with tears flowing, the other residents made their way to the front to wave her off.

Driving away, beeping the horn, Alf took hold of her hand and said 'It's going to be alright you know.'

'I know, just ignore me,' she said, completely choked with tears.

'I will look after you, like Tom would want,' he said, smiling at her.

'Thank you and I will look after you for Elsie too,' she said, squeezing his hand.

When they arrived, Will, Sarah and Lily had been there about an hour and were just getting the last bits out of the van.

'Why don't I help Sarah and Lily, while you go to get Alf's stuff and close up his house?' suggested Sylvie, carrying her suitcase into the cottage.

'Great idea,' they both replied and set off for Alf's.

Loading up his stuff and finally shutting the door, they both looked at each other.

'Who'd have thought, Mr Charlick, that this would ever be happening? When you think back to those nightmare brothers and family and how it all began, just goes to show you can never tell how things are going to turn out in the end can you?' said Alf, smiling. Locking his front door for the final time, he took a deep breath, wiped away the tears that had escaped and got in the van.

Arriving back at their new home finally, with everything now on board they both knew that this was how it was always supposed to be. And later on, sitting in the garden all together, tucking into their first takeaway from the local fish and chip shop in the village, and a glass of bubbly in hand, they all felt so content and happy. Sarah and Lily had picked a few of the flowers from the front and put them in a small glass in the middle of the table.

Out of nowhere, two of the most beautiful butterflies you have ever seen appeared and landed together on the flowers. And as Lily decided she might like to try and grab them, they flew off and disappeared. Like they were just sent to let them know that things were going to be alright now...

www.ingramcontent.com/pod-product-compliance
Lightning Source LLC
Chambersburg PA
CBHW030316080526
44584CB00012B/589